A DIFFERENT GOD

Louvain Theological and Pastoral Monographs is a publishing venture whose purpose is to provide those involved in pastoral ministry throughout the world with studies inspired by Louvain's long tradition of theological excellence within the Roman Catholic tradition. The volumes selected for publication in the series are expected to express some of today's finest reflection on current theology and pastoral practice.

LOUVAIN THEOLOGICAL & PASTORAL MONOGRAPHS
— 17 —

A DIFFERENT GOD

A CHRISTIAN VIEW
OF SUFFERING

by Kristiaan Depoortere

PEETERS PRESS
LOUVAIN

W.B. EERDMANS

Cover: Pietà by Anto CARTE (1886-1954),
Centre Hospitalier Universitaire Arthur Gailly, Charleroi, Belgium.

ISBN 90-6831-653-2
D. 1995/0602/1

TABLE OF CONTENTS

PART II

THREE ACQUITTALS OF GOD

PART III

A GOD OF POWER AND/OR OF LOVE?

FOREWORD

There are so many types of suffering. Pain has so many faces. If we want to deal with suffering, we have to start somewhere, from an unavoidably limited perspective. We cannot but start by focussing on one facet of suffering. The suffering persons we have in mind are the longterm ill, those still capable of contacts and relationships. They may reside at home or in a hospital. They are attended by helpers who are convinced that their work cannot be restricted to mere physical care.

Starting from this determinate perspective, we shall try to enlarge our view. Among human beings mere physical pain does not exist. Human beings react as a whole. Almost all human pain is total or global pain, covering different aspects of life. It embraces physical, psychic, moral, social, and often religious facets. Moreover, human suffering should be — and mostly is — shared suffering. We suffer because of and/or together with other persons. Suffering has an intersubjective dimension.

There is still more. Whether shared or not, suffering raises questions. These questions concern many things, but, ultimately, they are about life as such. Suffering interrogates life. It asks questions about our daily way of life, about its direction and its ultimate meaning.

At first glance our approach could seem too narrow: a sick person in his or her bed. However, the questions dealt with in a sickbed are timeless ones and concern every kind of human suffering and healing.

Nevertheless, we do not intend to deal with all dimensions of pain and suffering. Starting from the global human experience of pain sketched above, we shall try to focus the religious questions of the sense and nonsense of pain and suffering. Initially, however, the term "religious" is taken in its broad and etymological significance of *religare*, that is to say, to link, to bind, to refer to, to put into a relationship with some transcendent element. This general meaning of transcendence serves, however, only as a point of departure. One of the principal aims of our work is the clarification and specification of vague and impersonal images of God. This will bring us to the principal part of our study, which can be summarized in the following questions: Which images of God do suffering people have? Is there any link between particular images of God and the way people come to terms with pain and suffering? Are some images of God more helpful to this handling than others? What can we do with images of God which induce sick persons to resignation and passive acceptance? How can we disclose an image of God which helps the sick to struggle against suffering?

All these questions converge into one fundamental question: if there is a link between God and suffering — of whatever sort — who is this God?

Our considerations concerning the meaning of suffering and the different images of God are directly intended for people who guide suffering fellow humans: professionals as well as volunteers, pastors, and lay pastoral workers, nurses, doctors, and also visitors and relatives. Our work is only indirectly addressed to the sick persons themselves. This is because it is neither easy nor beneficial to fiddle with a sufferer's image of God while he or she is in the midst of suffering. Suffering and pain as such suffice. The sick persons' situations do not allow them to modify their images of God and confront the void which inevitably opens up. A change in one's image of God — in the event of one being necessary — should find place before suffering strikes hard. This is the reason why we have a second group of addressees in mind: all those persons who are involved in permanent education, in spiritual guidance or in different forms of catechesis in "normal" situations, where there is enough room to adjust images of God before crises intervene.

It is customary to dedicate a book to someone. I would like to dedicate this work to the nurses and the pastors who have shared with me their concerns for their sick and dying patients. I have learned from them so much about life.

Belgium, Leuven, November 1, 1994, Feast of All Saints.

PART I

SUFFERING PEOPLE

In this first part, entitled "Suffering People," we shall consider different aspects of suffering and develop an integral concept of suffering. Suffering, as an integral human phenomenon, disturbs all our relationships. Pain affects the relationship with our body; it distorts our contacts with the world and with fellow humans. Finally, suffering obliges us to ask compelling questions about human finiteness.

Following upon these reflections, the present chapter will offer a couple of basic principles which will guide us through the whole book. The first of these is our conviction that, in most cases, human beings are, at the same time, the authors and the victims of evil and that, consequently, we should avoid both the arbitrary accusation and the indiscriminate exoneration of suffering people. Our second basic principle is that we should never detach an attempt to attribute meaning to suffering from an unremitting fight against suffering. All too often, the attribution of meaning results in the cessation of the struggle against suffering.

Subsequently, we aim to develop some of the essential elements of the struggle against suffering. These include the courage to hear the real questions sick people ask, the courage to enter into a relationship, and the courage to break through the taboo of death and dying. It is only when we have arrived at a living solidarity, which involves protest as well as acceptance, that we can ask the question of the meaning of suffering and allow suffering to ask the question of God's existence.

1. AN INTEGRAL CONCEPT OF SUFFERING

At first glance, the most striking form of suffering in a hospital seems to be physical suffering. However, a closer look reveals that nearly every kind of physical suffering evokes psychic, social, and moral suffering. Jan Hendrik van den Berg describes how the different aspects of suffering and pain are intermingled.[1]

HEALTHY medically sound	SICK medically sick	RECOVERED medically recovered
On the level of the integral human experience		
spontaneous relationships	conflicting experiences	growing towards new harmony
	MY BODY =	
instrument	hindrance	partner
	WORLD =	
great territory	small territory	day-to-day values
	RELATIONSHIPS=	
understanding	incomprehension	understanding incomprehension
organization around the ego	isolation	solidarity
	FINITENESS =	
theory	living experience	core-life
little why's	too many why's	acceptance

Health, illness, and recovery certainly are medical phenomena. A doctor's diagnosis is, for the most part, accurate. But we must ask the question: are there not other aspects than those diagnosed by medical sciences? A person may well have an illness. But, he or she *is* ill, too. Illness is not simply something affecting the out-

---

[1] Jan Hendrik van den Berg, *Psychologie van het ziekbed* (Nijkerk: Callenbach, 1952).

side of our person. It is inside, too. I do not feel 39°C warm; I feel poorly. "I feel bad." I *am* ill. Health, illness, and recovery are integral phenomena. They concern the global human person. Generally, these integral experiences are congruent with the medical data, but this is not necessarily the case.

Let us take a closer look. To be in good health means to live comfortably — in relationship — with four important dimensions of human life: the body, the world, fellow humans, and finiteness. When one is ill, these four spontaneous harmonies become four areas of conflict.

The Body: From Docile Instrument to Hindrance

A healthy person enjoys a natural, spontaneous relationship with his or her body — a relaxed, somewhat nonchalant, and quite harmonious alliance. One can express this in somewhat dualistic terms by saying that one's body is a docile instrument. A more up-to-date formulation would be: I am my body.

Illness abruptly reveals the naïveté of such a view. Illness is a brusque confrontation with the fact that "I have a body." It is a breakdown in communication. It involves antagonism, perhaps even enmity. In any event, it involves disappointment. Before, when writing a letter, I thought "through" my arm, my fingers, and my pen to the sheet of paper, and the addressee. But this inflammation of my elbow hinders the running current between my thoughts and the sheet of paper. A man with a paralysed arm takes the sleeve of his pajamas, lifts up the "object," and says, "This one fails me." Illness changes our experience of the body.

Like illness, recovery is more than just a medical affair. An integral human recovery might sometimes differ from a medical recovery. A person can still be ill from a medical point of view and, at the same time, be on the way to an integral recovery. He or she has gone through the confrontation with suffering and pain, and almost everything has changed. The body is no longer a docile instrument. The experience of breakdown has made the body a partner. A partner is someone very close to me, someone familiar.

A partner is not, however, my-self. The experience of difficult days might bring about a more realistic view of this partner, and generate more respect for them. An integral recovery means a growth towards a new harmony. Perhaps resurrection (at least to some extent) can be conceived of as following upon this new harmony.

The World: The Shrinkage of a Territory

A sick person's territory shrivels to the dimensions of a bed sheet. The corridor nearly becomes terra incognita. Homecoming is the return to bed after a long journey to the toilet. Worse still, merely turning over in bed can become a major achievement. And the pillow must be precisely in that place, nowhere else. Sick persons can become incredibly attached to particular habits and practices, even to quirks. In a hospital this shrinkage takes on frightening proportions. Everyone penetrates into your territory; you wake up when "they" want it; you should be hungry when "they" command.

After such a confrontation the world will never be the same. Some people never get over it. Still others, however, discover a new harmony. Perhaps they have not recovered "medically." Nevertheless, in an integral human way they are enriched. Flowers become precious things, while a tree just outside the window represents the change of seasons. The sensation of laying in fresh sheets reminds one of one's childhood in a secure home. The confrontation with illness can make old things surprisingly new.

Fellow Humans: People who Leave me Behind

To be healthy means to be inserted into a network of relationships. Illness changes this network. Life goes on, but the sick person is left behind. He or she no longer belongs to the network. Some sick people become passive: "I am ill." Others become childish: "Would you, please, if possible, if you have a moment ..." There are too many thank yous: the subdued and submissive behavior brought about by powerlessness, defenselessness, and uncertainty. There may be a recurrent return to the discomforts of the surgery. And, if the illness is protracted, there may be the problem of the visiting hours: "I don't know any more what to say to my own wife. We never talked that long before, and now it's obligatory from 2:00 to 8:00." In the beginning there are many visitors — too many visitors and too many lengthy visits. There is so much news about home, the family and the work place, and the sick person feels interested. Gradually, however, he or she falls back on his or her own problems. It is as if the visitors are aware of this change. There are fewer visitors, and, if they come, they remain silent about the job: "He's been gone so long already that he won't know what I'm talking about. Maybe we hurt him by talking about the work place. It's better to keep quiet." The sick person tries to read the visitor's mind, and the visitor tries to read the sick person's mind. A vicious circle develops. Or the sick person feels suspicious: "What do they know about my situation?" There are feelings of having been replaced: "Yes, everything is all right at home." The concerned husband lies, and the mother feels still more superfluous and unneeded. Then again, there may be a trivializing optimism and indiscrete questions. Then there is the sick person in the next bed who volunteers: "If necessary, I can tell your story to the next visitor." There is a great gulf fixed between the bed-ridden and the able-bodied.

When a person recovers from a serious illness, many things have changed. Some patients leave behind the shame of being dependent and feel a new gratitude. Sometimes, relationships of true solidarity develop between patients. And one knows the faithful visitors. Relationships are sorted out during a stay in the hospital. Genuine relationships are confirmed or discovered. The loss of many "business-relationships" offers the opportunity for new ones. The sick person becomes milder. He or she understands the incomprehension of healthy people. Relationships change — little things become valuable, and things once deemed important pale in significance.

Finiteness: From Mere Theory to Rough Confrontation

From time to time, a healthy person asks questions about the fragility of life, especially "when the hatchet strikes closely" (François Mauriac). One quickly returns to current affairs, however.

A sick person, even when not terminally ill, lives through an acute experience of finiteness. Thoughts come crowding in after visiting hours and during the nights. Mortality becomes an existential experience. To be subject to complete narcosis means to abandon your life into the hands of other persons. Until today the rhythm of work and promotion pushed our finiteness far ahead of us. A healthy person is quietly aware of his or her relative irreplaceableness. However, this awareness is shaken by serious illness, and the awareness of replaceableness evokes radical finiteness. Not infrequently, there are experiences of guilt, both real and false. Or there is a primitive anxiety: "Illness is the consequence of guilt; illness is revenge;" "Why did this happen to me? Did I deserve this?"

Here, we are very close to religious questions in the broadest sense of the word: everything that concerns the foundations of one's existence in its ultimate links (*religare*). These are questions which reveal a much deeper conflict than the relationship with the body, with the world, and with fellow humans.

It is not the case that every person pronounces the word "God" quickly and consciously when confronted with a situation of distress. Nevertheless, He is the final addressee. These are all "religious" questions, even if they are not explicitly addressed to God. The "why's" are addressed to Fate, to Life, to Existence, but they always concern the profoundest depths, something or someone above me, with whom I have to strive and who escapes my grasp. A battle of this sort injures a person. Like Jacob, one is wounded by the struggle with that "angel" (Genesis 32:23-33).

To recover does not mean to have a ready-made answer to all these questions. The process of recovery starts when people "dare" ask questions. This means that they no longer flee from inevitable boundaries. There is an opportunity for a more integral harmony, whether or not one is a believer. Hitherto, one kept silent about dying. Now that one "knows" about it, every day can become more valuable, and the time that remains can be lived more intensely.

For Christians, this "processing" will be colored in a typical way. It will run through a solidarity with Christ, who has lived through the same conflicts: the conflict on the Mount of Olives when he pleads, "Father take this cup away from me!"; the conflict with his environment when the soldiers cast lots for his garments, and his disciples flee. We can read the Way of the Cross as a process of increasing isolation. Finally, there is the conflict with God Himself: "Father, why hast Thou forsaken me?"

Through such an experience of solidarity, a Christian can discover the epilogue of Jesus' story in a very living way: "Not my will, but Yours, Father." On the cross, Christ experiences a new kind of solidarity. The good thief becomes his companion, and the pagan official is the first of the new group of believers. Finally, the conflict with God issues in the words: "Father, into thy hands I commit my spirit." Then the Third Day dawns, Easter morning.

Between illness and recovery, there is much suffering. We began our description of suffering with physical pain in a hospital. Of course, this is only a fragment of the whole. We could have described psychic suffering — the lack of security, stability, and an affectionate milieu; in brief, the lack of love. We could have offered a description of anxiety as a social phenomenon, as Jean Delumeau has done.[2] With Paul Tillich,[3] we might have presented a sketch of culture and history and of three types of anxiety: the anxiety of fate and death, the anxiety of guilt and rejection, the anxiety of emptiness and meaninglessness.

We might consider suffering from a social perspective — the lack of esteem and self-actualization, the lack of social identity,

---

[2] Jean Delumeau, *Sin and Fear: The Emergence of a Western Guilt Culture, 13th-18th Century* (New York: Saint Martin's Press, 1990).

[3] Paul Tillich, *The Courage to Be* (London: Collins, 1952).

the themes of stress, competition and burn-out. In this instance, suffering is called discrimination or humiliation, individually or in group. We might have started from moral suffering: the pain of the denial of human rights, the suffering effected by every kind of apartheid, powerlessness in the face of structural injustice, pain at the suicide of a fellow man or woman, the suffering born of the disappearance of love, and so forth.

A number of authors insist on the typical human aspects of suffering. Human consciousness means that a person suffers more than an animal; the higher the consciousness, the higher the capacity for suffering. Still other authors connect human suffering with human desire. Because human persons desire — and what else do they desire more than happiness? — they suffer when their desire remains unsatisfied. The endlessness of desire means that human persons are capable of endless suffering. Do people suffer more today than in the past? Is it true that psychic pain has increased because contemporary men and women are more fragile and have more difficulty accepting the inevitable? Does social suffering increase because today's discrimination is more discrete and human resilience is weaker? The description of human suffering could be extended indefinitely.

2. HUMAN BEINGS: AUTHORS AND/OR VICTIMS OF SUFFERING

Is it possible to bring some greater order into the description of suffering offered above, by introducing the distinction between the kind of suffering which is undoubtedly caused by human beings, and the kind of suffering of which human beings are the victims? The following reflections will lead to the first basic principle of our approach to pain and suffering.

Without any doubt there is suffering which is caused by human beings, and of which human beings, both individuals and groups, are the direct authors. Classic theology deals with suffering brought about by sin: the suffering directly caused by fellow humans who are guilty because they are sufficiently free, and sufficiently aware of what they are doing.

At the opposite end of the spectrum, we find the suffering born of "nature". Human beings are not the cause of it — they are simply victims. Such suffering includes the suffering brought about by the catastrophes of nature; the suffering of innocent people; the fact that human beings have to die; matter's resistance to our labors; the fact that a choice involves a loss, and so forth. Of such suffering, Paul Ricoeur says, "This is not guilt, it is due to our finiteness."[4] This kind of suffering has no guilty author. It seems to be linked with the finiteness of being a human, and to be unavoidable. There is much room for reflection here, but one thing is clearly true: there is more suffering on earth than human beings cause.

In most situations, however, there is a mixture. Human beings — that is to say, humanity as a whole — are, at the same time, both the authors and the victims of suffering. Much suffering arises from the space between freedom and nature, between guilt and finiteness — suffering as a result of a finite freedom and an abused finiteness.

In classical theological terms, this is the suffering that is the fruit of original sin. In some languages (for example, Dutch and German) the term original sin is translated as *hereditary* sin. This is not a very successful translation. Nevertheless, this complex limit-concept accents an element that is absent in the notion of *original* sin, one which concerns the border region between liberty and finiteness. The term "hereditary" suggests finiteness, which is neutral from an ethical perspective. However, the term "sin" designates a responsible freedom.

Even Genesis 2:4-3:24 refers to that border region. There is undoubtedly a free human initiative: the transgression of the inter-

---

[4] Paul Ricoeur, *Philosophie de la Volonté: Finitude et Culpabilité. Tome I: L'Homme faillible & Tome II: La Symbolique du mal* (Paris: Aubier-Montaigne, 1960); English translation of Tome II: *The Symbolism of Evil* (Boston: Beacon Press, 1969).

dict to eat from the tree of knowledge of good and evil (in other words, not to have recognized that human beings are not allowed to define good and evil — at least not with absolute autonomy). On the other hand, there are some elements in the story which designate the limitation of human liberty. The snake is a symbol of the evil which is "already there", a symbol of a tradition of bad choices, into which humans are born. There is Eve who does not so much symbolize femininity as human frailty in general, and the fact that human beings might be seduced.

This is the duality of the concept of original sin: a tradition of evil choices in which human beings continue to make evil decisions. Human beings join and reaffirm the structures of evil, discrimination, injustice, and exploitation. Human beings practice their limited liberty within the framework of social habits which function as a well-worn path, and which channel individual choices in a direction that causes suffering. In a certain sense, original sin means solidarity in evil which provokes suffering.

The recognition that most suffering arises in this border region between guilt and finiteness is of great significance. If we too readily admit that suffering is caused by an abuse of liberty, we contradict daily experience: there is much suffering which has no responsible author. Even more, we accuse other people without reason, or we impose an unbearable burden of guilt on ourselves. This overly simplistic reduction runs from Pelagius to Rousseau (human beings are naturally good, but society breaks them), and is also evident in some forms of Marxism (it suffices to alter substructures in order to change society). All of these reductions overestimate guilt, and underestimate suffering and evil.

On the other hand, the hasty acknowledgement that suffering is to be reduced to nature or to the finiteness of human beings leads to a deterministic pessimism which paralyses the struggle against evil and pain.

In most situations of suffering, there is shared responsibility. There is a link between aridity in the Sahel, centuries-old deforestation, and international investment. If we reduce desertification to a question of meteorology, we abandon human responsibility.

This is also true of famines in the Nordeste of Brazil, of earth-quakes and criminality, and of many epidemics.[5]

3. REFLECTING ON SUFFERING WHILE STRUGGLING AGAINST IT

Our second basic principle is closely linked to what has been said above. It consists of a permanent distrust of every theory which seeks to adopt an impartial position, and refuses to look for the causes of concrete situations of suffering. It is a distrust of every philosophy or theology which seeks to "cleanly" manage suffering, and is intolerant of the experience of powerlessness. It is a distrust of every system which seeks to "explain" suffering but forgets the suffering person. It is, finally, a distrust of every technical or purely medical analysis of suffering.

Hearing the Nocturnal Questions

As we explained above, meeting suffering people and healing them involves two dimensions. There is, first, the task of curing them by making use of all the possibilities of technical medicine. Secondly, there is the need to care for them by means of a more integral human approach, which takes into consideration all of the psychic, social, moral and religious aspects of pain and suffering, and which devotes special attention to questions of meaning. These are those questions addressed to Life, to the Cosmos, to Humanity, to God — those questions concerning happiness, since suffering always raises questions about happiness.

During the day, patients plagued by headaches ask: "Can I have a pill?" At night, however, the question becomes: "Why me? What did I do to deserve this?" Integrated care hears these

---

[5] Gisbert Greshake, *Der Preis der Liebe: Besinnung über das Leid* (Freiburg im Breisgau: Herder, 1979); rev. ed.: *Wenn Leid mein Leben lahmt: Leiden, Preis der Liebe?* (Freiburg im Breisgau: Herder, 1992).

nocturnal questions and creates space for them. Still, we must not play off professionalism against humanity. We must not juxtapose intravenous tubes full of antibiotics in a hospital, and soup at home. Nevertheless, it is important that the increasing technicality of medicine be accompanied by a proportionate effort to hear the nocturnal questions of the patients. There is special training to teach nurses how to lift up patients in order to change their bedclothes; there is, however, relatively little training in how one can help patients answer questions of meaning. Suffering and pain expose forgotten regions of human life. Not infrequently, these are regions where questions of culpability lie buried: an ancient feud, neglected religious practice, a daughter-in-law one has never accepted, a maladjusted image of the Church and of God, and, in the final analysis, the last question of all: "Have I loved enough?"

To struggle against suffering means to hear these questions, to take them seriously, and, by listening, to convert this anxious story into a love story. This requires time and energy, because an anxious story is afraid of itself. It is expressed indirectly. It is masked, as in the parable of the watch. Every morning a widow opens her door at nine o'clock because her rather obsessive neighbor leaves his house to buy a newspaper at precisely that hour. Every morning she asks him the time, and every morning he answers, "Nine o'clock, dear neighbor; have a good day." At Christmas, the neighbor buys her a watch. A week later she is dead.

When sick people ask, "What time is it?," they often give expression to their medical condition: their inability to sleep, their pain, their denial of their disease. Initially, we answer, "It is nine o'clock". But then we buy watches: we pray with them, we speak about the anointing, or about the weather. We tell them, "Next week you can go home;" or we avoid this room in the hospital; or we observe that "she has gone into a coma, which is best for her, since she was so worried ..."

In reality, we, too, we are afraid of her questions, and of her loneliness and meaninglessness. Elizabeth Kübler-Ross tells the story of a student nurse with leukemia:

I am dying. I write it to you who are, and will become, nurses .... I am dying — but no one likes to talk about such things. In fact, no one likes to talk about much at all. We're taught not to be overly cheery now, to omit the 'Everything's fine' routine, and we have done pretty well. But now one is left in a lonely silent void. With the protective 'fine, fine' gone, the staff is left with only their own vulnerability and fear. The dying patient is a symbol of what every human fears and what we each know, at least academically, that we too must someday face. What did they say in psychiatric nursing about meeting pathology with pathology to the detriment of both patient and nurse? And there was a lot about knowing one's feelings before you could help another with his. How true. But for me, fear is today and dying is now. You slip in and out of my room, give me medications and check my blood pressure. Is it because I am a student nurse, myself, or just a human being, that I sense your fright? And your fears enhance mine. Why are you afraid? I am the one who is dying! I know you feel insecure, don't know what to say, don't know what to do. But please believe me, if you care, you can't go wrong. Just admit that you care. That is really for what we search. We may ask for why's and wherefore's, but we don't really expect answers. Don't run away — wait — all I want to know is that there will be someone to hold my hand when I need it. I am afraid. Death may get to be a routine to you, but it is new to me. You may not see me as unique, but I've never died before. To me, once is pretty unique! You whisper about my youth, but when one is dying, is he really so young anymore? .... If only we could be honest, both admit of our fears, touch one another. If you really care, would you lose so much of your valuable professionalism if you even cried with me? Just person to person? Then, it might not be so hard to die — in a hospital — with friends close by.[6]

Entering into a Relationship

To struggle against suffering means to look for the courage to be a sister or a brother, to find the courage to enter into a relationship with the dying person, and, in a certain (but very real) sense, to die with the dying. It is only for those who love that suffering and death become real.

---

[6] Elizabeth Kübler-Ross, *Death, The Final Stage of Growth* (Englewood Cliffs: Prentice-Hall, 1975) 25-26.

Dorothee Sölle affirms that the victory over suffering and its causes can only be achieved through solidarity. Suffering isolates. Moreover, it originates in, and is aggravated by, isolation. Coping with pain only starts where people share the experience of their suffering fellow humans. No one can attribute meaning to his or her own suffering except through fellow humans. Without solidarity suffering has no meaning, or at least no meaning which can be called human.[7]

Dorothee Sölle provides a schematic summary of her ideas:[8]

PHASE I	PHASE II	PHASE III
mute	lamenting	changing
speechless	able to speak	organizing
moaning	psalmic language	
animal-like wailing	rationality and emotion	rational language
ISOLATION	COMMUNICATION	SOLIDARITY
autonomy of thinking, speaking and acting lost	autonomy of experience (can be integrated)	autonomy of action that produces change
objectives cannot be organized	objectives utopian (in prayer)	objectives can be organized
reactive behavior		active behavior
dominated by the situation	suffering from the situation and analyzing it	helping to shape the situation
POWERLESSNESS	ACCEPTANCE AND CONQUEST in existing structures	ACCEPTANCE AND CONQUEST in changed structures

In the first stage — according to Sölle — suffering descends upon human beings and assails them. People are overrun, dumb, and mute. They can only groan and moan. It is almost an animal

---

[7] Dorothee Sölle, *Suffering* (Philadelphia: Fortress Press, 1984).
[8] Ibid., 73.

lament, which cannot find expression in words. It is, as it were, an explosion of feelings. Suffering is an intruder. Human beings are the victims of robbery. All their relationships are cut off. The suffering person is isolated; he or she is a stranger to other persons and to him or herself. The autonomy of thought, speech and action is destroyed. The sufferer cannot distance himself or herself from this unexpected assault. His or her only desire is to disappear into this abyss, into the depths of death. There are only two possible outcomes: to be broken or to find someone to talk with.

There is no second stage after this first archaic stage unless the suffering person meets someone who listens. If someone listens, the moan becomes complaint. In the beginning it is a bitter word, a complaint against injustice, an assault directed against everyone, even against the compassionate listener. But, precisely here, muteness becomes language. In his or her complaint, the suffering person achieves a distance from the pain. The word is the first attempt to organize overwhelming suffering. It is not yet a rational or effective organization, but it is already a more articulate expression of emotions. Sölle calls this complaint "psalmic language":

> The worker's objectives are not organized as yet; they still appear — as in prayer — as utopian wishes. What is depicted is really suffering, but it is no longer at the stage of submissiveness. I think of his language as 'psalmic language' not so much in respect to a literary genre as to specific elements of language, such as lament, petition, expression of hope. Also characteristic is the emphasis on one's own righteousness, one's own innocence .... This is the kind of opportunity for expression that the liturgy used to offer in the past. Liturgy at one time served to give voice to people in their fears and pain, and in their happiness.[9]

The suffering person remains in this second stage unless there are other people who are ready to collaborate in order to change the situation.

In the third stage complaint changes into articulate speech. The content of suffering is expressed. Language has become real com-

---

[9] Ibid., 71-72.

munication. Other fellow humans understand and respond. There is solidarity instead of isolation. The conviction prevails that people who act in solidarity against evil will overcome it.

> The way leads out of isolated suffering through communication to the solidarity in which change occurs .... That sort of thing is conceivable only in the context of a group of people who share their life — including their suffering — with one another. One of them can then become the mouth for the others, he can open his mouth 'for the mute' (Proverbs 31:8). Liturgies of that kind do not abandon people to apathy.[10]

The Taboo of Death and Dying

Sölle is not afraid of the confrontation with suffering. However, many other systems which seek to attribute meaning to suffering consist of attempts to flee from it, and to protect the self against pain. According to Sölle, this attitude characterizes contemporary society.

> One wonders what will become of a society in which certain forms of suffering are avoided gratuitously, in keeping with middle-class ideals. I have in mind a society in which a marriage that is perceived as unbearable quickly and smoothly ends in divorce; after divorce no scars remain; relationships between generations are dissolved as quickly as possible, without a struggle, without a trace; periods of mourning are 'sensibly' short; with haste the handicapped and sick are removed from the house and the dead from the mind .... From suffering nothing is learned and nothing is to be learned. Such blindness is possible in a society in which a banal optimism prevails, in which it is self-evident that suffering doesn't occur .... An inability to perceive suffering develops, not only one's own, through indifference, but especially the suffering of others .... In the equilibrium of a suffering-free state the life curve flattens out completely so that even joy and happiness can no longer be experienced intensely. But more important than this consequence of apathy is the desensitization that freedom from suffering involves, the inability to perceive reality. Freedom from suffering is nothing other than a blindness that does not perceive suffering .... Walls are erected between the experiencing subject

[10] Ibid., 74.

and reality. One learns about the suffering of others only indirectly
— one sees starving children on TV — and this kind of relationship to the suffering of others is characteristic of our entire per-
ception .... We no longer touch the warmth and coldness of the
sick body. The person who seeks this kind of freedom from suffering quarantines himself in a germ free location.[11]

We find the same warning in the books of Philippe Aries.[12] Van
den Berg also sketches contemporary "narrow-mindedness". We
live as if suffering and death did not exist. Things were totally different in the Middle-Ages, with its lepers and their rattles, the pil-
grimages and processions, the last anointing with the bell in the
streets, the bells tolling death. Reflecting on our clean hospitals,
van den Berg observes that death has been banished from these
places of recovery. We all try to hide death even from the dying.
The doctor gives morphine, certainly if the death threatens to be
painful. However, at the same time, he brings about what everyone
secretly wants, namely, that the illness overcomes the sick person
while he or she is unconscious.

In the same framework, the author depicts the contemporary
disguising of pain:

> The cemetery is no longer situated in the middle of the town or
> around the church. It has been moved outside, a green place with
> trees and flowers, hidden, covered. The passer-by assumes it is a
> country estate, not the kingdom of death. Only those who travel by
> train can see the graves directly. The railway is a remarkable artery
> which allows us to see towns as they really are, without frills,
> directly, in their moving and shameful nakedness .... Psychologi-
> cally speaking, it is dangerous to banish illness and death from
> daily life. Where this happens, the transitoriness of life is changed
> into a veiled, and therefore dangerous threat. Illness and death
> become catastrophes which may unexpectedly fall upon us at any
> moment. Contemporary human beings can be compared to the
> young Buddha who had been educated far from every human suf-
> fering, and became extremely vulnerable for everything that did

[11] Ibid., 38-39.
[12] Philippe Aries, *Western Attitudes toward Death from the Middle-Ages to the
Present* (Baltimore: John Hopkins University Press, 1974); *L'Homme devant la
Mort* (Paris: Seuil, 1977).

not fit his artificial paradise. We do not live with the realities of
our existence, and precisely because of this denial, reality forces
itself upon us as undefined anxiety.[13]

4. THE ENCOMPASSING QUESTION OF MEANING

The core questions are not: how do we avoid suffering? How
do we flee from suffering? How do we become less vulnerable?
The price paid for these solutions is the amputation of too great a
part of reality. A person who becomes less sensitive to suffering
becomes, at the same time, less sensitive to love.

The Challenge of the Courage to Be

From a Christian perspective — albeit not exclusively so —
the first question is: how do we strive against suffering? The
reverse side of this question is: what can we do to promote happiness? How can we stimulate love and life? The third question
is: where and how can we help in the bearing of unavoidable
suffering? Where can we be Simon of Cyrene? These three
questions are the most important ones. They challenge our
courage to be.

The courage to be includes the acceptance of reality, with its
invincible evil, as a situation offering us the opportunity to build
something human, and to develop humanity. This active answer to
suffering demands resignation and the recognition that human
power is limited. This resignation, however, is not a negative attitude. On the contrary, it is the necessary condition for the struggle
against fatality, and the discovery of happiness in limited creative
activity. Without this kind of resignation, a human person will perish in fruitless revolt or in distant despair and discouragement.
One need not approve of evil and suffering, in order to concede
that much of what civilizations have produced has been born of

---

[13] Van den Berg, *Psychologie van het ziekbed*, 17-18. See also Johannes B.
Brantschen, *Warum lässt der gute Gott uns leiden?* (Freiburg: Herder, 1986).

the creativity inspired by the challenge of suffering. The French poet Paul Claudel has written, "*Le mal est dans le monde comme un esclave qui fait monter l'eau.*"

Protest and Acceptance

It is our conviction that suffering is meaningless, at least in the first instance. This means that we have to fight against suffering with all our possibilities, especially when it is a matter of innocent suffering. To use the word "meaningless" is to indicate that suffering should not exist. This affirmation is of capital importance because an overhasty attribution of meaning to suffering leads to a cease-fire in the battle against suffering, and to a kind of approval or justification of suffering. The immediate attribution of meaning and the insensitivity to concrete suffering constitute a vicious circle. It is as with Kübler-Ross's description of dying. Acceptance differs from passive resignation. Acceptance includes a certain courage to live and to protest against death. This protest changes acceptance into a human act. In the same sense we have to affirm that suffering must be fought.

But this is not all. We have not simply insisted that suffering is meaningless. This would be risky, both from a Christian and from a human perspective. The risk is that this might encourage despair or paralysis. Again, we can use the comparison with the process of dying: protest and acceptance keep each other in a sound equilibrium. As regards suffering in general, abandonment keeps protest healthy and human. Daring to express a "nevertheless" despite everything, protects the suffering person from despair. This "nevertheless" means the invincible hope in something or in Someone who transcends suffering.

In other words, the main question is: how do we revolt against superfluous and unnecessary suffering which can be eliminated, and, at the same time, accept and bear together unavoidable suffering, while we seek its elimination? Here, too, anger and acceptance are twins; protest and acceptance support one another. If we could offer suffering people such a "relative meaning," it would be a kind of help for them. It would allow us to be Simon of Cyrene for them. Human beings are searchers after meanings. Situations which have a meaning are a little bit more tolerable. Hence, Harold Kushner compares the pain of giving birth with the pain provoked by passing a kidney stone.[14] The same intensity of pain is born in a different way because of the greater or lesser degree of meaningfulness of the pain. As Victor Frankl observes,[15] human beings are in search of a meaning for everything, especially for suffering,

Attribution and/or Discovery of Meaning

In our quest for the meaning of things, we encounter an enormous philosophical question. As far as the attribution of meaning is concerned, we are able, broadly speaking, to distinguish two major poles around which philosophical systems develop.

On the one hand, we find those systems which consider human beings as absolute givers of meaning. This view of humans as autonomous beings is found in atheistic existentialism and in Marxism. However, these views offer too little when it comes to the question of suffering. They cannot give any meaning to individual suffering. Here, personal sacrifices run the risk of being absorbed by the sacrifices required for the development of the System.

On the other hand, there are most of the religious views of life. According to these, human beings are more the finders than the founders of meaning. Meanings come from "elsewhere," and encounter human beings who discover them. These views run the risk of saying too much about suffering. They run the risk of attributing meaning too directly, and thereby of minimizing suffering, and of concealing human tragedy. Harold Kushner refers

---

[14] Harold Kushner, *When Bad Things Happen to Good People* (New York: Avon Books, 1983) 63-64.

[15] See Viktor Frankl, *Man's Search for Meaning: an Introduction to Logotherapy* (New York: Pocket Books, 1963); *The Unconscious God: Psychotherapy and Theology* (New York: Simon and Schuster, 1975) *Das Leiden am sinnlosen Leben. Psychotherapie für heute* (Freiburg: Herder, 1978).

to Thornton Wilder's *The Bridge of San Luis Rey*. In Peru five people die when a bridge collapses. A spectator analyzes the lives of the victims. The result is the bitter conclusion that they all died when they did, precisely because they had just righted a wrong in their personal lives and refound their way. Perhaps it was an appropriate time for each of them to die. However, Kushner goes on to inquire about 250 victims of a plane crash. Forty years later the same Wilder wrote another novel, *The Eighth Day*. Therein he describes the world as a beautiful woven carpet. Looked at from the front, the tapestry is harmonious. Viewed from behind, however, it is a chaos of threads, and gives every appearance of being quite arbitrary. Wilder concludes that life and suffering can be compared to the tapestry. Looked at from underneath, from a limited human point of view, life seems arbitrary and lacking in design, not unlike the underside of the carpet. But looked at from outside, from God's standpoint, every twist and knot has its place in a grand design. Kushner, however, asks if there is indeed a front side, if we do not see it?[16]

We shall return to this problem in our second part, when we reflect on different images of God in relation to suffering. We shall endeavor to bring both aspects closer together, and to value the human person as both a founder and a finder of meaning.

5. SUFFERING AND THE QUESTION OF GOD

Suffering as the Question of God's Existence

Suffering raises the question of God's existence because suffering hides God. The whole relationship with God is affected by suffering. In a poem which treats of the Holocaust, the Dutch author, Marnix Gijsen, compares God to Ilse Koch who made lampshades out of human skins: "Is God's heart a rock? He offers us cancer, blindness, and so on. He is terribly inventive when it comes to

---

[16] Kushner, *When Bad Things Happen to Good People*, 17-18.

misery and disease. If I were to stand before His throne, I would ask Him, how could You see all this and bear it?" Of course, suffering raises the question of God's existence for believers as well as unbelievers. On his sickbed, Romano Guardini, the famous Catholic theologian, confided to a friend: "At the Last Judgment I will not simply allow myself to be questioned. I will ask questions too. I expect that the Angel will not refuse to answer the question to which I never found an answer, neither in any book nor even in the Scriptures, neither in dogma nor in my own theology: why, God, are there such terrible detours to redemption? Why do innocent people suffer? Why is there guilt?"

God's Existence and the Aggravation of the Problem of Suffering

Suffering raises the question of God's existence (Is there a God, if such suffering is possible?). But if He exists, there are still more severe questions about suffering (How can He allow all this to happen?). Suffering raises the question of God's silence. It is a theme dealt with by the Japanese author Shusaku Endo in his novel *Silence*. A missionary is forced to be present at the torture of his faithful (17th century). He feels the conflict between the faithfulness of his tortured peasants and his own experience of a silent God. Finally, the missionary accepts the proposal of the executioners: he can save the lives of many faithful if he forsakes his faith — even merely formally. All he has to do is to kick the Cross. So he does, to save lives. The samurai, however, with psychological perspicacity, realized that this rite amounted to much more than a formal, external gesture. It was a symbol of the missionary's anger with his silent God. The missionary lost his faith, and his dreams of a glorious martyrdom got bogged down in a life of bitter banality.

This story is much more than a mere tale in the fashion of those which begin with the celebrated words, "once upon a time." In the confrontation with suffering, the faithful might revolt against their God, especially when their God is not an idea but a living reality. This even occurs among those believers who are of the opinion that they critically purified the concept of divine providence. When distress, disease or death hit them, their partner or their children, a vital reaction takes their rationalized knowledge by surprise. Involuntarily they engage in something inconceivable to rational minds: they hate God. A disappointed love-bond is reversed into a hatred which is still a life-bond. However, a believer cannot maintain this bond of resentment with God. Either his or her trust is purified, or he or she kicks the Cross.

There is probably another reason why belief in God aggravates the problem of suffering. The person who lives according to the Gospel knows that his or her love should become wider and deeper. He or she knows that a Christian cannot be perfectly happy as long as other people suffer or are exploited. An egoistic "I feel OK" cannot satisfy a believer.

A God of sym-pathy?

The decisive question is this: does God's existence change my life? Not simply my life as such, but my life there where it is hit by suffering? We have obtained at least one element of an answer: we cannot accept an image of God which paralyses the fight against suffering and leads to passivity or fatalism. We shall not speak "about" suffering without striving against it, that is to say, without sym-pathy — without suffering together with others.

Out of this basic question more precise questions arise: on what can this attitude of sympathy be founded? Can we base this attitude on an appropriate image of God? Is our God a God of sympathy with suffering people? If the answer is yes, then many things change. As Jacques Maritain wrote: "Suppose ... that God suffers with us, and even much more than we do, about the evil which ravages the earth. Then many things would be different, and many souls would be appeased."[17]

---

[17] Jacques Maritain, as quoted by François Varillon, *La souffrance de Dieu* (Paris: Le Centurion, 1975) 15.

There is still another step: there is not only God's suffering together with us. The whole story would be totally different if God's sympathy were powerful too; if His sympathy were so powerful that it could stop this endless succession of sufferings; if His sympathy were effective; if the Gospel really did continue after 3:00 p.m. on Good Friday; if there were a guaranteed promise of a Third Day for our world, too.

PART II

THREE ACQUITTALS OF GOD

At the heart of the Christian view of the world stands the affirmation that God is the beginning and the end of everything. He is the creator of the universe. There is no other principle beside Him: "We believe in one God, the Father, the Almighty, maker of heaven and earth, of all that is seen and unseen." In addition to His might, the Christian faithful assert God's goodness. This double-concept of God throws the problem of suffering into very sharp relief. How can we combine the following elements: God is the creator of everything; He is good; there is so much suffering? Why? Perhaps He only permits suffering? Again, why? In both cases, can such a God be called a good God? Or do we misunderstand the word "good"?

We shall meet these questions in this part of our study. We shall discuss three attempts to resolve these problems, all of which seek to free God from the *guilt* of suffering. We deliberately use the word "guilt." It is not a question of whether or not God is the *cause* of suffering. According to the three conceptions to be considered, God does cause suffering, either directly or indirectly. Nevertheless, "He has good intentions." A distinction is made between being morally responsible for suffering, and being the cause of suffering. This is the idea which links the three attempts. Although God is aware of suffering, He is not guilty of it. The three conceptions to be considered are three pleas on behalf of God. The guilty one is the human person. Suffering is a consequence of irresponsible human behavior. Human behavior should be corrected by suffering. God does precisely this, respectively, as a fair Judge, as a supreme Educator, and as an inscrutable God. We shall provide a brief description of each conception, and then reflect on its values and disvalues.

1. GOD AS A FAIR JUDGE

A World of Merits and Demerits

The first attempt to acquit God of guilt for human suffering involves the representation of God as a fair Judge. The world view behind this portrait is often very matter-of-fact, very realistic, and indeed, almost materialistic: it is a world of merits and demerits. The whole world can be grasped and understood in terms that are reminiscent of bookkeeping or accountancy: all profits and all losses are quoted and noted. The relationship between God and human beings is characterized by terms such as insult-appease-ment, guilt-expiation, crime-punishment. In theological terms, this finds expression in the notions of atonement, expiation, and ransom. The principle of this world-order is retribution or repayment. God is the guardian and the guarantor of this system of immanent justice. He is a Judge. Occasionally, the intervention of saints is sought to stop God's punishing hand. This concept of God can be very resistant. It is evident in claims such as: "Aids is a punishment designed by God."

The Plea of Job's Friends

The Book of Job, which dates from between the 5th and the 3rd century B.C., deals with the meaning of suffering. Etymologically, "Job" could mean, "Where is the father?" Though this interpretation of the name may not be exact, it is not without meaning: "Where are you, Father, when I suffer?"

The original story is well-known. It is called the "framework." It is written in prose, and includes the chapters 1 and 2 and 42:7-17. In heaven there is a kind of audience and Satan (*dia-bolos*, the one who divides, the opposite of *sym-bolon*) meets God. Satan maintains that Job does not fear God "for naught" (1:9), and proposes to God: "Put forth thy hand now, and touch all that he has, and he will curse thee to thy face" (1:11).[1] Satan receives God's permission to test Job's honesty. Job loses everything — possessions, sons and daughters. However, "Then Job rent his robe, and shaved his head, and fell upon the ground, and worshipped. And he said, 'Naked I came from my mother's womb and naked shall I return; the Lord gave, and the Lord has taken away; blessed be the name of the Lord" (1:20-21).

In the next audience Satan asks God for another chance. Up until now, Job's own life has not been at stake. "May I go on and touch his bone and his flesh?" Job is covered with sores from head to foot. His wife protests, "'Do you still hold fast your integrity? Curse God, and die!' But Job said to her, 'Shall we receive good at the hand of God, and shall we not receive evil?' In all this Job did not sin with his lips" (2:9). At the end of the story the Lord restores the fortunes of Job. He gives him twice as much as he had before.

This is the essence of the classic legend. However, a poetic story has been inserted between chapters 2 and 42. This poem tells of Job's wrestling and his coming to terms with suffering. Here, there is an element of "sins with his lips" — a real crisis of faith. Chapter 3 is the great complaint:

> Let the day perish wherein I was born,
> and the night which said,
> 'A man-child is conceived.'
> Yea, let that night be barren;
> let no joyful cry be heard in it.
> Let the stars of its dawn be dark;
> let it hope for light, but have none,
> nor see the eyelids of the morning.
> Why did I not die at birth,
> come forth from the womb and expire?
> Why is light given to a man whose way is hid,
> whom God has hedged in? (3:3,7,9,11,23)

[1] All biblical texts are taken from the Revised Standard Version of the Holy Bible, Catholic Edition (London: The Catholic Truth Society, 1966).

Job shares the height of the crisis with his three friends - Eliphaz, Bildad, and Zophar (chapters 4-27). In turn they respond, and they all say the same thing: God is fair, and Job is guilty, even if he does not remember the reasons why he is guilty: "He that mischief hatches, mischief catches."

> Think now, who that was innocent ever perished?
> Or where were the upright cut off?
> As I have seen, those who plough iniquity
> and sow trouble reap the same. (4:7-8)

But Job protests against Eliphaz. He is disappointed by the latter's theories:

> My brethren are treacherous as a torrent-bed
> as freshets that pass away.
> In time of heat they disappear;
> when it is hot, they vanish from their place. (6:15,17)

And Job attacks God Himself:

> Am I a sea monster,
> that thou settest a guard over me?
> When I say, 'My bed will comfort me,
> my couch will ease my complaint,'
> then thou dost scare me with dreams
> and terrify me with visions.
> If I sin, what do I do to thee,
> thou, watcher of men? (7:12-14,20)

Then Bildad speaks: "You have left your God, that's why you suffer now!"

> Such are the paths of all who forget God;
> the hope of the godless man shall perish.
> His confidence breaks in sunder,
> and his trust is a spider's web.
> Behold, God will not reject a blameless man,
> nor take the hand of evildoers. (8:13-14,20)

And so on. In turn, the friends plea on behalf of God. Again and again, Job expresses his disappointment, even with God. But no believer can endure these attacks against God. In the midst of an

angry attack against his friends, Job displays a kind of provocative
trust: if God lives, He will prove it!

> If indeed you make my humiliation
> an argument against me,
> know then that God has put me in the wrong,
> and closed his net about me ....
> Why do you, like God, pursue me?
> Oh that my words were written!
> Oh that they were inscribed in a book!
> Oh that with an iron pen they were graven
> in the rock for ever!
> For I know that my Redeemer lives,
> and at last he will stand upon the earth;
> and after my skin has been thus destroyed,
> then from my flesh I shall see God,
> whom I shall see on my side,
> and my eyes shall behold,
> and not another.
> My heart faints within me! (19:5-6,22-27)[2]

Job's friends do not understand how deep Job's faith still is.
They accuse him of godlessness and predict still worse if he continues in this fashion. When Job asks his friends to listen to his
complaint and to hear what is behind his words, one is reminded
of the experience of modern sufferers and those who accompany
them on their journey: "Listen carefully to my words, and let this
be your consolation. Bear with me, and I will speak, and after I
have spoken, mock on" (21:2-3). Consolation all too frequently
turns into accusation and subtle apportioning of blame. We tell the
lonely to look for more contacts, or to find a good friend. But this
is precisely the problem. It is this which they are not capable of
doing. Parents worry about their children. In spite of their efforts
and good intentions, their children choose alternative ways of life.

---

[2] See G.F. Händel's *Messiah*: "I know that my Redeemer liveth." Redeemer is a
well-known term in the Jewish Torah. If a member of the community loses all his
possessions, his family has to redeem his debts. Similarly, if an individual dies
without children, a member of the deceased husband's family must marry his
wife. When Job calls God a "redeemer," he has this sense of the term in mind:
the closest member of the family whose duty it is to intervene.

We then ask the parents if the education they provided was not perhaps too weak or too rigorous? Once again, however, this is the heart of the matter. Good intentions do not insure good results. Persons feels depressed, and we answer them that they have their husband, their wife, their children. We tell them that they take things too seriously, or that they are too concerned for themselves, or that they should forget their own problems. If they could just do this, their problems would be solved. All these are Eliphaz-answers.

In a later stage, Job feels fear of the God of his friends who, nevertheless, remains, at once, tremendous and fascinating:

> Oh, that I knew where I might find him,
> that I might come even to his seat!
> I would lay my case before him
> and fill my mouth with arguments.
> I would understand what he would say to me ....
> Therefore I am terrified at his presence;
> when I consider, I am in dread of him.
> God has made my heart faint;
> The Almighty has terrified me;
> for I am hemmed in by darkness,
> and thick darkness covers my face. (23:3-5,15-17)

At the insistence of his friends, Job makes another examination of conscience (chapter 31). Still, he does not change his mind: I did nothing wrong. In this manner, Job's friends gave the eternal explanation for suffering: you are guilty, maybe secretly, maybe unconsciously. There is no exception to this universal law: a virtuous life is rewarded; a wicked one is punished. If you are suffering, you are being punished. If you are being punished, you are guilty, since God is a fair Judge. This retributive vision finds expression in such phrases as: "why did I deserve this?"; or, in regard to others: "they've lived the life of Riley...;" "they live from one day to the next, and up to now they've been lucky;" or, "she had an accident, on her way home from church no less; or, "God will get them!" (The assumption is that the divine book-keeper will mete out punishment in a perfectly balanced fashion).

In fact, as Heinz Zahrnt argues, Job's friends play the devil's game.[3] The devil wants to prove that people never believe freely. They believe with a view to their own profit. Every faith has its basis in egoistic motives, such as the longing for happiness. Karl Marx called this kind of belief the "opium of the people," since it is nothing more than the search for a happiness which has no foundation in reality. The background to such belief is a mixture of the fear of punishment, and the need for protection. The God who corresponds to this human attitude is at once Accuser and Consoler. Later theological reflection creates a moralistic God who rewards the good, and punishes the bad. The moral law of retribution is linked with the idea of divine providence: God rules over the world by means of sanctions and rewards, by the threat of punishment, and the promise of protection.

The Value of the Perspective

The fact that this view on suffering has continued through the centuries indicates that it contains some valuable elements. There is a link between unjust behavior and suffering. Injustice provokes suffering. Human persons acknowledge the legitimacy of a law which punishes those who practice injustice (at least when it concerns injustice done to them). According to Kushner, this view of retribution survives because it is an orderly system. It explains, somewhat, the relationship between guilt and suffering. At least superficially, this explanation seems to be correct: nobody is perfect. Consequently we all merit some "punishment."[4] By means of this theory, those who suffer are able to exercise a certain intellectual control over uncontrollable reality, even amidst their despair. Their suffering seems to be somewhat comprehensible. There is, after all, enough sin in everyone's life to "legitimate" punishment.

---

[3] Heinz Zahrnt, *Wie kann Gott das zulassen? - Hiob: Der Mensch im Leid* (Munich: Piper, 1985) 32-33.

[4] Kushner, *When Bad Things Happen to Good People*, 9-10.

The Disvalues of the Perspective

Despite the presence of some valuable elements, this view of suffering is ultimately inadmissible. Among its many flaws, it is unfair both to human beings and to God.

In those cases where there is a question of real guilt, suffering can rightly be considered as a punishment. One cannot, however, maintain that suffering is always the consequence of an error, and always a punishment. The most convincing proof of this in the Old Testament is the figure of Job.[5] Job continuously denies the penal character of his suffering: he has done no wrong. This denial culminates in the so-called purification oath (31:35-37). In Jewish jurisprudence a purification oath is an act by which the one presumed guilty challenges his accuser to reveal the hidden guilt and to give proofs of it. If the accuser cannot demonstrate guilt, the accused person is discharged. This is what happens to Job (42:7-8): Job you are right; Your image of Me, your God, was better than that of your friends! Please pray for them!

Even daily experience contradicts the notion of an intrinsic link between guilt and penance. People who lead a guilty life are not always punished. In any case, if there is a link between guilt and punishment, it is clearly not of the order discussed above. The victims of injustice, or those who protest against it, are the ones who are punished. Jesus Christ is the most convincing example of this fact.

The image of God as a cold judge is unfair to human beings. This concept of God supports and stimulates the idea of resignation devoid of resistance in the face of suffering. It encourages resignation, not active acceptance. It paralyses human initiative. It does not allow for the distinction between suffering that can (and thus must) be fought, and suffering that is beyond all human possibilities of control. Not infrequently, such an explanation of suffering issues in self-torturing attitudes. A vicious circle develops: trans-

---

[5] John Paul II, *Salvifici doloris: On the Christian Meaning of Human Suffering* (Washington: United States Catholic Conference Publications, 1984) no. 11. The text is also contained in *Origins* 13 (1984) 609-624.

gression brings guilt, and guilt breeds the expectation of retributive punishment. Sometimes, however, punishment does not find
place, or the guilt is not expiated by suffering. In such a case, the
person who desires redemption from guilt can look for more
severe penalties. Still, when "punishment" comes, it is not
accepted without revolt.[6] Kushner rejects this view because people
run the risk of losing their God. They are angry with the God who
punishes them. At the same time, however, they realize that this is
really a sin. Hence, they hate both God and themselves, and they
are left alone.[7]

The image of a cold judge is also unfair to God. Such a vision
is only compatible with the image of a purely moralistic God — a
God who tries to set the world right by means of punishment and
reward. Job's friends appeal to a God who is greater than human
beings. Their God is indeed greater. He is not, however, different.
The God whom they defend is nothing more than a magnified
human father. Job's friends put Sigmund Freud in the right
when he asserts that the Christian God is only a "greater" earthly
father, One who accuses and punishes, and consoles and protects
in the fashion of human beings. The longing for such a father is
the root of all human religious needs. The religious person
behaves before God like a child. A child fears its father, and seeks
his protection. According to Freud, a religious person remains
dependent on this childish image of a menacing and protective
father. Unable to leave this secure shelter, such a person is incapable of adulthood. Religious men and women need an "education towards reality." Such an education will lead towards adulthood. The God whom Freud combats is precisely the God of Job's
friends: the "greater" father who protects and chastises, rewards
and punishes, sends suffering and takes it away. He is the father of
their early youth, whom they both admire and resent, trust and
fear. Job combats this God by his faith and his behavior.[8]

[6] André Knockaert, "Catéchèse de la souffrance: présupposés pédagogiques,"
Lumen Vitae 37 (1982) 310.

[7] Kushner, *When Bad Things Happen to Good People*, 10.

[8] Zahrnt, *Wie kann Gott das zulassen?*, 33-34.

The God designated by Job and revealed by Jesus is not merely "greater" than human beings. He is different. Jesus is the image of a God who breaks through the accounting system, a God who continuously offers new — undeserved — opportunities, a God who does not fit in with any human scheme. The way in which God breaks through all-too-human insights is evident in the parable of the workers of the eleventh hour (Matthew 20:1-16) in one shocking verse: "Do you begrudge my generosity?" (20:15). God breaks through the closed system of merits and demerits. He is not a God of revenge; He is not a God of bookkeeping retribution. An encounter with a God who is neither a copy of our needs and longings nor an amplification of a childish father-figure, will be the most serious test for everyone who wishes to achieve an adult faith.

According to Elie Wiesel in *Le Procès de Shamgorod*, it is only the devil who defends the image of a retributive God. In a Jewish community many inhabitants have been killed in a cruel raid. The survivors plan a ritual in which they want to take God to court. All the parts are cast, except one: the defender of God. Finally a stranger agrees to play the role. He defends God in such a marvelous manner that the survivors ask him to put in a good word for them, and to ask God for protection because new raids are expected and the defender seems to be close to God. Then the defender reveals his identity — he is the devil. He alone has the nerve to defend God, and to plea on His behalf in the face of human suffering. Kushner quotes an Iranian proverb: "If you meet a blind man, kick him; why should you be kinder than God?"[9]

2. GOD AS A SUPREME EDUCATOR

Medicinal Punishment

The image of God as a supreme Educator is a step forward. Suffering is still a punishment, but is now a medicinal one. Suffering

---

[9] Kushner, *When Bad Things Happen to Good People*, 87.

challenges human beings to conversion, or to a better way of life. Pain is a bitter pill but it heals people. In this view of things, suffering is no longer a kind of automatic revenge. It is, instead, a test or a purification. We encounter this view in certain popular expressions: "God tests His best friends;" or, "God does not impose unbearable burdens." In this context Kushner quotes Harriet Sarnoff Schiff in *The Bereaved Parent*. A clergyman says to a mother who has lost her child, "God never sends us more of a burden than we can bear. God only let this happen to you because He knows that you are strong enough to handle it." The mother answers, "If only I was a weaker person, my child would still be alive."[10] Sometimes this view of things is extended into the afterlife: "If we have to endure this here on earth, the reward will be the greater;" or "You will have a very good place in heaven..."

God: Wounder and Healer

The idea of a God who chastens and reproves us for our good is not absent from the Bible. The framework of Job (chapters 1-2 and 42) reveals this idea. Although it is Satan who chastens Job, God knows about it, and allows him to do so. Eliphaz, one of Job's friends, argues in this way:

> Behold, happy is the man whom God reproves;
> therefore despise not the chastening of the Almighty.
> For he wounds, but he binds up;
> he smites, but his hands heal. (5:17-18)

In the Book of Wisdom this concept is quite clearly evoked:

> For though in the sight of men they were punished, their hope is full of immortality. Having been disciplined a little, they will receive great good, because God tested them and found them worthy of himself; like gold in the furnace he tried them, and like a sacrificial burnt offering he accepted them. (3:4-6)

In the New Testament, the Letter to the Hebrews contains the following reflection:

[10] Ibid., 25-26.

For the Lord disciplines him whom he loves, and chastises every
son whom he receives. It is for discipline that you have to endure.
God is treating you as sons; for what son is there whom his father
does not discipline? If you are left without discipline, in which all
have participated, then you are illegitimate children and not sons.
(12:6-8)

Internal Transformation of the Punishment

Although he does not explicitly deal with our topic, Paul
Ricoeur, in *The Symbolism of Evil*, illustrates the evolution that
takes place between the image of God as a fair Judge and the
image of God as a supreme Educator. When God is conceived of
as a Judge, blind terror and anxiety prevail. When God is conceived of as a supreme Educator, human beings search for a
deeper meaning to suffering and punishment.

In a first step, human beings seek a just and proportionate punishment. The object is not wild vengeance but retaliation in the
Old Testament sense: only one eye for an eye and one tooth for a
tooth: "If a man is punished *because* he sins, he *ought* to be punished *as* he sins."[11] The idea of retribution is still present
(because), but it is already enriched by the idea of proportion (as).

In a second stage, fear-on-the-way-to ethics expects a punishment to have a meaning. In a certain sense, the punishment should
restore the disturbed order. Revenge should not be merely destructive. Rather, the destruction involved should restore, repair, and
redress. Punishment acquires the meaning of penance. The other
side of fear is the admiration for the order of the whole: "In
demanding that a man suffer justly, we *expect* the pain not to have
only a limit, but a direction — that is to say, an end."[12]

This search evokes a third moment: "If the *demand* for a just
punishment involves the *expectation* of a punishment which has a
meaning in relation to order, this expectation involves the *hope*
that fear itself will disappear from the life of conscience, as a

[11] Ricoeur, *The Symbolism of Evil*, 42.
[12] Ibid., 43.

result of its sublimation."[13] In this way Ricoeur sketches a slow evolution from the first image of God to the second one. But will fear ever disappear from our social life?:

> The abolition of fear appears to me to be only the most distant goal of ethical consciousness .... It is not the *immediate* abolition but the *mediate* sublimation of fear, with a view to its *final* extenuation, which is the soul of all true education .... Much is learned through fear and obedience — including the liberty which is inaccessible to fear. There are steps that cannot be dispensed with without harm. Certain forms of human relations, the relations that are properly speaking *civic*, cannot, perhaps, ever get beyond the stage of fear. One can imagine penalties that afflict less and less, and amend more and more, but perhaps one cannot imagine a state which has no necessity to make law respected through the threat of sanctions, and which can awaken consciences that are still unrefined to the notion of what is permitted and what prohibited without the threat of punishment .... Hence, the abolition of fear could only be the *horizon*, and, so to speak, the eschatological *future* of human morality. Before casting out fear, love transforms and transposes it .... The fear of not loving enough is the purest and worst of fears. It is the fear that the saints know, the fear that love itself begets. And because man never loves enough, it is not possible that the fear of not being loved enough in return should be abolished. Only *perfect* love casts out fear.[14]

The Values of the Perspective

There are at least three constructive aspects of this vision: suffering as a stimulant; suffering as an alarm; and suffering as the breaking open of an egoistically closed life.

Sometimes suffering and distress function as stimulants. Sufferings may incite human creativity if people manage to transform the impediment into a springboard. Brantschen tells an African story. Ben Zadok is an evil boy, angry with a palm in an oasis. In order to damage the tree, he lays a heavy stone on the top of the palm. Because the tree could no longer grow upwards, it grew downwards and pushed its roots deeper and deeper into the

---

[13] Ibid., 44.
[14] Ibid., 44-45.

ground. When a period of drought occurred, it was the only tree to survive. "Thank you, Ben Zadok, your charge has made me stronger." Resistance may — sometimes — incite creativity. The most beautiful works of art are carved in the hardest stone. Is it true that there were fewer nervous breakdowns during the World Wars than after them? Some psychologists claim that spoiled children have a very low 'frustration threshold' and are more vulnerable than other children. Sometimes superficial things may lose their (overvalued) meaning in the confrontation with suffering. Simone Weil writes, "We need a view of the world, with empty places so that (the real) God may fill them up."[15] Dorothee Sölle calls Christ "both sweet like honey and bitter."[16]

Sufferings may function as an alarm, in the fashion of dizziness which can prevent a fall by giving the illusion of a fall before it really takes place, Scheler asserts.[17] Headaches, stress, and even shame point to deeper things — they are affective warnings.

Sufferings may open up a self-centered existence towards fellow humans. Nikos Kazantzakis describes such a process in his novel, *Greek Passion*. By way of preparation for a passion play during Holy Week, the parish priest of a quiet Greek village designates people to play the roles of Jesus, Peter, John, Jacob, Judas, and Mary Magdalene. Then, the serenity of the village is disturbed by the arrival of the fleeing population of a neighboring Greek village burnt down by the Turks. The local priest wishes to protect his own village, and sends the beggars away. In the meantime, however, the actors chosen by the priest begin to incarnate their roles, and to behave in the fashion of the original characters. Hence, Manolios, the future Jesus, disagrees with the priest's decisions, and, together with Peter, James and John, cares for the beggars, thereby dividing the village. Eventually, a few days before Easter, Manolios is killed.

The novel touchingly illustrates the way in which sufferings and setbacks can break open egocentrically closed lives, at least in

[15] Simone Weil, *La Pesanteur et la Grâce* (Paris: Plon, 1948) 21, 46.
[16] Sölle, *Suffering*, 100-101.
[17] As cited in Kushner, *When Bad Things Happen to Good People*, 62-63.

some cases. Some authors compare this (potentially) beneficial aspect of suffering to the pain of giving birth. In their opinion, every step towards greater humanity includes pain, at least as a form of taking leave of a former stage. Only through pain can new life arise. On occasion, this is certainly the case. Pain and suffering may break open a defensive bastion around the ego: I have to call for help. This is one of the paths which bring people together. In one of his books Victor Frankl tells about a Jewish scientist who is arrested by the Nazis, and sees how his scientific works are burned before his eyes. After a period of great depression, he works through his own pain and helps other people to bear their suffering: "They have not lost books but children."

The Disvalues of the Perspective

The educational value of suffering cannot be the final word. Despite its constructive dimensions, this view, for the most part, does justice neither to God nor to humans.

First of all, this interpretation of suffering does not stand the test of reality. Perhaps someone may grow by suffering (or grow through suffering) but the risk of not growing at all is much greater. While some people are purified by suffering, many others are broken or embittered. Can suffering serve as a stimulant? Only if the challenge is not overwhelming, and the person challenged is possessed of sufficient strength. Can suffering function as an alarm? Perhaps, but must one catastrophe serve as the alarm for a succeeding one? Can suffering serve as a kind of liberation? Perhaps; much more frequently, however, suffering makes people shrivel up and close in on themselves. While some people are purified by suffering, most are broken, embittered, or gravely hurt.

Moreover, there is no honest proportioning of suffering. Often there is an excess of suffering which cannot be justified by any educational result.[18] Do you pay for the deepening of your life by the death of your child, Kushner asks? What kind of pedagogy

---

[18] Zahrnt, *Wie kann Gott das zulassen?*, 34-35.

does God practice when He punishes and frustrates His children without any explanation?[19]

The risk of passive resignation is as great as the possibility that an individual will courageously put his or her trust in God. One might well claim that this or that suffering is part of a divine plan or that it will be compensated by our heavenly reward. To my mind, however, this is simply scandalous as a principle of divine pedagogy. Who can honestly call innocent suffering "God's pedagogy"? I cannot recognize the God of my father and my mother in this view. I see only a distant master, or the director of a puppet theater, or even an executioner. "It is unacceptable and even inconceivable that God tests human beings by means of all kinds of sufferings, and examines them in this way in order to let them acquire the grades needed to move on to the next class."[20]

Moreover, this view of things has been too frequently invoked to support the abuse of power by the mighty of the world. Mighty tyrants have argued in this way to justify and legitimize their cruelty, and have even described suffering as an educational device.[21] John-Paul II acknowledges that this concept has biblical supports, but he asserts that it is not the last word, "To discover the real answer to 'why suffering', we have to look at the revelation of the divine love."[22]

3. AN INSCRUTABLE GOD

God: Greater than our Heart

There is a third view which aims to acquit God of the guilt of human suffering. This view evidences much more respect for human pain than other theories. We can illustrate this alternate

---

[19] Kushner, *When Bad Things Happen to Good People*, 23-25.
[20] Zahrnt, *Wie kann Gott das zulassen?*, 36.
[21] Ibid., 37-38.
[22] John-Paul II, *Salvifici Doloris*, no. 11 and no. 13.

view by means of expressions such as the following: "God's ways are inscrutable;" "What God does is well done;" "God writes straight on crooked lines." All these expressions are characteristic of this third vision: a profound faith in God's goodness and omniscience; a strong trust in Him who is much greater than our human heart.

Job's Theophany

We find the biblical foundations of this view in the last part of the poem in Job. After the purification oath, God appears on the scene. In the whirlwind He addresses Job. God is the Almighty who meets a human being, and God neither argues against Job's self-defense nor blames him for his revolt. He offers a glance behind the scenes and gives Job a foretaste of His mighty plans. God does not allow Himself to be questioned. He does not render an account of His deeds. On the contrary, the Almighty demands of Job that he render an account of his behavior:

> Who is this that darkens counsel by words without knowledge?
> Gird up your loins like a man, I will question you,
> and you shall declare to me.
> Where were you when I laid the foundation of the earth?
> Tell me, if you have understanding.
> Or who shut in the sea with doors,
> when it burst forth from the womb;
> when I made clouds its garment,
> and thick darkness its swaddling band,
> and prescribed bounds for it, and set bars and doors,
> and said: Thus far shall you come, and no farther,
> and here shall your proud waves be stayed?
> Have you commanded the morning since your days began?
> Has the rain a father, or who has begotten the drops of dew?
> From whose womb did the ice come forth?
> Can you bind the chains of the Pleiades,
> or loose the cords of Orion?
> Do you know when the mountain goats bring forth?
> Do you observe the calving of the hinds?
> Shall a faultfinder contend with the Almighty?
> He who argues with God, let him answer it.
> (38:2-4,8-12,28-29,31; 39:1; 40:2)

Job answers the Lord:

> Behold, I am of small account;
> what shall I answer thee?
> I lay my hand on my mouth.
> I have spoken once, and I will not answer;
> twice, but I will proceed no further. (40:4-5)

But the Lord continues:

> Gird up your loins like a man;
> I will question you, and you declare to me.
> Have you an arm like God,
> and can you thunder with a voice like his?
> Behold Behemoth, which I made as I made you;
> he eats grass like an ox.
> He is the first of the works of God;
> let him who made him bring near his sword!
> Can you draw out Leviathan with a fishhook,
> or press down his tongue with a cord?
> Will he make many supplications to you?
> Will he speak to you soft words?
> (40:7,9,15,19; 41:1,3)

Then Job gives way, and the poem concludes:

> I know that thou canst do all things,
> and that no purpose of thine can be thwarted.
> Who is this that hides counsel without knowledge?
> Therefore I have uttered what I did not understand,
> things too wonderful for me, which I did not know.
> I had heard of thee by the hearing of the ear,
> but now my eye sees thee; therefore I despise myself,
> and repent in dust and ashes. (42:2-3,5-6)

God is not a partner of equal value to Job. He shows him how
well all things have been created. It is incomprehensible to Job, for
God does not fit the framework of comprehension. Job keeps
silent. God does not blame Job for isolated sins but for a faulty
basic attitude: for seeking to justify himself in front of the Creator,
and for adapting his trust to his understanding. It was because Job
began to lose his trust in God, that he interpreted suffering as a
divine assault. When God appears, Job discovers how different

God is. Job is not given an explanation. Through suffering, however, he meets a God who is merciful in spite of everything. The
theophany is not only an exhibition of God's power, and God is
not only the creator. He also cares for everything He has created.
This appears from verse 40:9: "Have you an arm like God?" This
"arm" is well-known in the Bible. It is not God's arm which
strikes and hurts, but the arm which saves. This arm is God's
protest against tyranny and terror. The theophany is more a
demand for trust-in-spite-of, than a vision of creation. God's
appearance in the storm is much more an invitation to vital confidence in Someone than a rational explication of something. Job
grasps this. He does not say at the end, "Now my eye has seen it",
but, "Now my eye sees Thee" (42:5).

After the theophany the framing story continues, and Job gets
back all that he had lost. Job has learned that the immense sea of
suffering should not be a hindrance on the way to God. He accepts.
He does not understand. There is a kind of admiring dumbness at
the end of the story: an acceptance of non-understanding coupled
with a trusting leap. The leap is towards a "different" God. It is the
radical and painful discovery of God's otherness.

The Values of the Perspective

This approach to the problem of suffering has rightly found its
defenders down through the centuries. It is, indeed, possessed of
several valuable elements.

First of all, suffering always remains a mystery. A mystery is an
invitation to enter, and to try to understand from the inside. It is
not a problem that can be circumscribed, analyzed, and "solved".
Not everything can be explained; not everything can be changed.
Many answers to the "why-questions" are nothing but abstract
theories.

Suffering confronts human beings with their helplessness.
When reality does not conform to our wishes, it is important that
people do not lose all confidence or give way to paranoia. As
Heinz Zahrnt observes:

Job recognizes God's presence in the fact that human beings do
not dispose of their existence. This primordial experience in every
human life has two sides. On the one hand, there is the dark, inim-
ical experience of threat and of the limitation of life; on the other
hand, there is the kind, friendly experience of a guarantee of full-
ness of life. People live both aspects simultaneously. There is the
realization that they do not dispose of their own lives, that more is
needed for their happiness than what they themselves are able to
do. Hence, they realize that their life runs the risk of radical failure. However, there is also the surprising experience that this
'more' is given, that what they cannot dispose of is granted to
them. Hence, they realize that their lives can turn out well.

In this manner Job puts his trust in God without presuppositions or
conditions. He is impelled neither by the fear of punishment nor by
the need for protection nor by the hope of a reward. Job commends
himself to a God who simply exists and is there. He does this
freely and with necessary abandon .... Job has faith but no vision
of the world. In the final analysis, this is a religion of true being,
not of merely feeling happy.[23]

"Thy will be done" is an essential part of a faithful attitude. It
is not necessarily an expression of passive resignation. On the contrary, where these words translate an intense trust, new life and a
new struggle can arise, even in the most impossible situations. It is
not insignificant that Luke places these words at the beginning of
his Gospel (where Mary says, "Let it be done unto to me according to Thy word" 1:38) and near its end (when Jesus, on the
Mount of Olives, prays, "Not my will, but Thy will, be done"
22:42). The beginning and the end of Jesus' life are framed, so to
speak, by the words, "Thy will be done". Such a "Thy will be
done" is related to the Hebrew word "Amen." It is the equivalent
of, "Nevertheless, Thou art trustworthy and veracious. That is
why I persevere." Such a belief in God's impenetrable goodness
does not so much allow one to understand suffering, as to with-
stand it, to bear it, and to come through it. Such a faith offers one
the opportunity to cross a sea of suffering, and to grasp the hand
which is extended over the abyss of evil. "Thy will be done" can

---

[23] Zahrnt, *Wie kann Gott das zulassen?*, 56-57.

signify the courage to go on saying "You", in spite of everything. Incomprehensibility and meaningfulness are not necessarily contradictory concepts.

The most valuable element of this view is its demolition of the notion of a "useful" God. For Job, religion "produces" nothing, neither profit nor loss. Distress is not always the bill for guilt. Justice does not guarantee happiness on earth. By means of this insight, Job supersedes the creed of his faithful friends. This is why his faith in God is not destroyed by Freud's criticism of religion. For Job, religion does not insure the fulfillment of unfulfillable desires. Job has painfully endured Freud's "education towards reality". He has become an adult, and a believer. He has met his God. He has experienced God as He is, different from human beings. In Job's faith, analogical and harmonizing thinking about the relationship between God and human beings has been shipwrecked. The God whom Job discovers is "unpredictable but not irresponsible."[24] He is who He is, different from human beings.

The Disvalues of the Perspective

Even this much richer view of the relationship between God and suffering cannot be allowed to be the final word, however. It is not without its flaws.

This vision, too, could culminate in the denial, the banalization, and the bagatellization of evil: "We are not able to grasp the course of the world; we are too tiny, too insignificant." This attitude could bring us dangerously close to demobilization in the struggle against suffering. Suffering certainly is a mystery, but this description should not encourage us to abdication or abandon the struggle against it.

Boethius (450-524), the last representative of the Roman era and the first representative of the Middle Ages, gave expression to the view which denies the tragedy of suffering. While he was

---

[24] Ibid., 58.

awaiting his execution, he wrote *De Consolatione Philosophiae*.
Therein, Lady Philosophia consoles him. In response to the question of how God can permit evil and suffering, Lady Philosophia
answers that Boethius suffers from blindness. God does nothing
wrong. He is simply good. Evil does not exist. Nor do evil persons. What is evil recedes from the source of goodness and disappears into nothingness. As the next chapter will show, Boethius'
ideas exercised tremendous influence during the medieval period
and long afterwards.

If the present image of an inscrutable God blocks the human
struggle against suffering, it is unfair to humanity. In the Middle
East, camels are sometimes called "Abu eyyub, Dad Job". They
are symbols of non-resistance and of the incapacity for revolt. This
is the heart of Abel Herzberg's critique of (a modern fellow-sufferer of) Job in *Three Red Roses*. Job gave way too quickly. The
author writes a letter to Job and blames him for having stopped his
trial. God should be taken to court again. God has to answer the
charge of the worthless, the childless, the fatherless and the moth-
erless, the damned, the oppressed, and all the lonely persons of
this world.

This image of God, with its great emphasis on His incomprehensibility, is unfair to God, too. In the words of Blaise Pascal
(1623-1662), this is "the God of the philosophers not the God of
Abraham, Isaac, and Jacob." Ultimately, the God of the Book of
Job remains distant, a somewhat authoritarian Creator, the One
who — when all is said and done — transcends human suffering.
Our God is not only the Almighty Creator. Above all, He is a God
of Love, and He answers the questions we ask not only with
words, but with His life. This life is called Jesus of Nazareth.

PART III

A GOD OF POWER AND/OR OF LOVE?

The pivotal conflict involved in the religious interpretation of suffering concerns the relationship between God's power and His love. Nevertheless, the entire Christian tradition has attributed these two characteristics to Him. Innocent suffering, however, seems to change these two attributes into contradictory terms.

We begin our discussion of this problem with Leibniz's classic theodicy. Our opening considerations are entitled, "God is All-Powerful — What about His Love?" Leibniz's theodicy is a rationalistic attempt to situate human suffering in the framework of God's plans for reality as a whole. Leibniz' view is very clear, but not sym-pathetic. The following consideration begins at the other end of the spectrum: "God is Love — What about His Power?" Unlike Leibniz, Harold Kushner provides an interpretation of suffering which stays very close to reality. It is almost the story of his personal life and suffering. Our third series of considerations are entitled "The (Im)potency of Love." This consists of an attempt to overcome the dilemma between power and love. Is power loveless, and love powerless, or is there something like the power of love?

1. GOD IS ALL-POWERFUL — WHAT ABOUT HIS LOVE?

The Trilemma of Theodicy

The Latin author, Lactantius (4th century) provides a precise formulation of Epicurus' claim that there is an opposition between God's power and His goodness. Lactantius expresses the view of his Greek predecessor — which he subsequently refutes — as follows: The opening question is, "Why does God not prevent human beings from suffering?"

> God either wishes to take away evils and he cannot, or he can and does not wish to, or he neither wishes to nor is able, or he both wishes to and is able.
>
> If he wishes to and is not able, he is feeble, which does not fall in with the notion of God. If he is able to and does not wish to, he is envious, which is equally foreign to God. If he neither wishes to nor is able, he is both envious and feeble and therefore not God. If he both wishes to and is able, which alone is fitting to God, whence, therefore, are there evils, and why does he not remove them?[1]

This is the trilemma of theodicy. It would be almost entertaining, if it did not concern such a horrible reality. Whether or not other logical formulations of the trilemma are conceivable, this one illustrates the perplexity of human reasoning in light of suffering.[2]

God as All-Powerful, All-Good, and All-Wise

Throughout history, people have sought to resolve the trilemma. Gottfried Wilhelm von Leibniz (1646-1716) continues to stand as a monument in this regard. In 1710 he published his *Essais de Théodicée sur la bonté de Dieu, la liberté de l'homme et l'origine du mal*.[3] Since then, the word theodicy has been used to mean the justification of God with respect to the human scandal of the history of suffering and evil.

Leibniz starts from two basic principles: on the one hand, he maintains that the world and human beings have been created by a

---

[1] Lactantius, *De Ira Dei* 13. We employ the English translation, *The Wrath of God*, in *Lactantius: The Minor Works* (Washington: The Catholic University of America Press, 1965) 92-93.

[2] Edward Schillebeeckx, "The Mystery of Injustice and the Mystery of Mercy: Questions Concerning Human Suffering," *Stauros Bulletin*, no. 3 (1975) 9.

[3] We have used the English translation, *Theodicy*, ed. D. Allen (Ontario: J. Dent & Sons, 1966).

perfect and good God who cannot have created evil; on the other hand, on the basis of his Christian conviction, Leibniz refuses to ascribe evil to a counter-divine principle of equal value. Consequently, he concludes that evil is not "something;" is not a "substance," but a "lack of goodness," an "almost nothing".

And who is responsible for this lack of goodness? According to Leibniz, human beings are responsible, because they freely contradict God's plans. What does God do in response? God does not positively will evil because this would be in flagrant contradiction with his goodness. On the other hand, it is not true that God does not will evil because if this were the case, there would not be suffering because He is almighty. The only solution is that God permits evil and suffering, in the cause of a higher goal (*"Nec vult Deus malum, nec non vult, sed permittit."*) Finite human beings, however, cannot grasp this higher goal and the all-encompassing view according to which everything meaningfully suits everything. God is not only all-powerful and all-good but, also, all-wise.

According to Leibniz, God has created the best of all possible worlds, a Universe where everything has its place, where lesser things are at the service of higher ones, worse things at the service of better ones, and the latter at the service of the best ones. If this world were not the best of all possible worlds, new internal contradictions would arise: either God did not know what the best world was — which would be in contradiction with His wisdom; or God knew it, but was not capable of creating it — which would be in contradiction with His power; or God knew it, but would not create it — which would be in contradiction with His goodness.

The answer to the question of whether God could have created a world without suffering is clear. "Indeed," Leibniz asserts, "God could have done so, but it would not have been a better world." If one specifies that the world one has in mind is "a better world for the sick, the poor, and the oppressed," Leibniz asks, "What is better, and for whom?" According to Leibniz, the Universe forms a complete and perfect whole. Its different parts are well-balanced, *harmonia praestabilita*. The Universe is the work of an intelligent Creator. This harmony applies to everybody and to every era.

Within this framework, Leibniz situates evil and suffering. Everything has its appropriate place within the best of all possible worlds. Physical evil or suffering is inherent to corporeality which feels pleasure as well as pain. The place an individual person occupies in the whole system also determines the measure of physical evil he or she undergoes. As a punishment or as a means of education, suffering is beneficial. Moreover, there are fewer pains than joys. However, human beings regard joys as self-evident. They therefore overlook them, and do not appreciate them enough. Actually, suffering endured with patience and faithfulness is bearable, Leibniz asserts. Moral evil or sin is a necessary dimension of human freedom and self-determination. Evil is permitted by God — not positively intended — and without evil there would be no good. Moreover, evil may add to good, if it is overcome by human beings.

The unlimited wisdom of the Almighty, together with his immeasurable goodness, mean that, on the whole, nothing better could exist than what God has created. Everything is in the most perfect possible harmony. If something in God's works seems to be blameworthy, one should accept that one does not know enough about it. A wise man or woman who could grasp the truth would conclude that there is no greater happiness than to serve God, to love Him, and to trust in Him.[4]

All that remains for the individual is to adopt an attitude of *metanoia*, or conversion, to abandon narrow-mindedness and to reconcile himself or herself with the pre-given world-harmony. According to Leibniz, this involves loving God in His goodness, believing in His wisdom, and trusting in His omnipotence.

---

[4] Gottfried Wilhelm Leibniz, *Causa Dei asserta per iustitiam eius, cum caeteris eius perfectionibus, cunctisque actionibus conciliatam. Sive synopsis methodica tentaminum theodicaeae*, 46-48, *Opera Omnia I*, ed. L. Dutens (Cologne-Berlin, 1789).

solely as a means to a greater end. A human being is an end in himself [or herself]."

Kant is not the only thinker to protest against this kind of rationalization of suffering. Such a theodicy is nothing more than "a clever cerebral argumentation, one which assists the sufferer about as much as a lecture on hygiene or on the chemistry of food would help someone who is hungry or thirsty", Hans Küng writes.[10] Karl Lehmann expresses the same idea as follows: "Nowadays we bridle at the notion of a 'higher harmony' as a means of explaining the evil and suffering in the world .... There has been a theological misuse of human suffering which weighs heavily upon us today: 'All pain comes from God's hand; the root of sickness is sinfulness; only in the Kingdom of God will complete health be found; suffering is a unique opportunity to mature inwardly; pain is God's sublime pedagogy for obstinate humanity' .... What has become problematic is not the attempt to cast light upon suffering in a personal and existential way but the subsequent theological system-building which produces a distinct impression of a lack of respect for real pain, or indicates a merely abstract compassion for it."[11] Erich Zenger observes that, "Suffering is not a theoretical problem which is capable of being comprehended intellectually. Pain can never be merely understood; it is a situation which can only be undergone, through a human, Christian, believing praxis .... If we look carefully, we will notice that reflections upon suffering generally arise not from the actual arena of suffering but rather from the tribunes. Down in the arena people suffer, perhaps amid complaints and cries of distress; maybe, despite all this, they still praise God, but they scarcely reflect upon their suffering. In the painful arena suffering is not a problem, it is a reality."[12]

If speculative theory represents one end of the spectrum, a praxis of resistance represents the other. "Suffering must not be understood; it must be strenuously fought." The only direct experience

[10] Hans Küng, *Gott und das Leid*, Theologische Meditationen, 18 (Einsiedeln: Benziger, 1967) 18.
[11] Karl Lehmann, *Jesus Christus ist auferstanden* (Freiburg: Herder, 1975) 28.
[12] Erich Zenger, *Durchkreuztes Leben* (Freiburg: Herder, 1976) 14, 25.

The Political Context of Theodicy

Leibniz's *Essais de Théodicée* became a best-seller in Enlightened Europe during the 18th century. From Leibniz onwards, and especially in the work of Hegel (1770-1831), we encounter a very optimistic philosophy which justifies evil and very nearly dismisses it as "almost nothing". What human beings, in their short-sightedness, regard as evil and suffering is, in reality, nothing more than a relative moment, used by the Spirit to guide history of humankind to its fulfillment.[5]

This view has been both the source and the motor of political absolutism. By means of an appeal to this so-called enlightened view, the violence and the brutal egoism of tyrants have been justified as instruments at the service of progress. This rationalization of suffering has given birth to ideologies which mercilessly incorporated suffering into programs designed to achieve humanity's and society's future. Joseph Stalin — to cite but one example — justified the starvation and deprivation of millions of peasants, and the suffering of millions of convicts in slave-camps, by portraying it as a sacrifice in the cause of a new future for humankind. A death in a family is a drama, Stalin remarked, but, to the leader of the future society, thousands of dead are mere statistics. Within the framework of such a rationalistic ideology of progress, the person does not count and personal suffering hardly has a meaning.

From Theodicy to Anthropodicy?

Many philosophers have protested against this sort of theodicy. They include David Hume (1711-1776) and François-Marie Arouet, alias Voltaire (1694-1778). In response to the earthquake of Lisbon in 1755, which cost 30,000 lives, Voltaire wrote his *Poem on the Disaster of Lisbon* (1756): "*Philosophes trompés qui criez: 'Tout est bien', Accourez, contemplez ces ruines affreuses,*

[5] Georges De Schrijver, "From Theodicy to Anthropodicy," *God and Human Suffering*, ed. Jan Lambrecht & Raymond Collins, Louvain Theological and Pastoral Monographs, 3 (Leuven: Peeters, 1990) 100-102.

Ces débris, ces lambeaux, ces cendres malheureuses!" ("Deceived philosophers who cry, 'Everything is fine'; come and look upon these terrible ruins, this debris, these rags, these tragic ashes.") We should delete any reference to God in explaining suffering, Voltaire said. God is not responsible. He is *l'Horloger Suprême*, the Great Watchmaker. He started the world moving, but He no longer intervenes (deism). Jean-Jacques Rousseau (1712-1768) drew the consequences: human beings must account for themselves. When faced with events such as the earthquake of Lisbon, we must not resort to speculation but ask why humans pack together in thousands, in places as small as Lisbon. Here we see the beginnings of a movement away from a merely theoretical theodicy towards a concern for concrete action, a trend which has continued till today. According to Edward Schillebeeckx,[6] our contemporary culture has promoted human beings to lords of history and makers of the future. Consequently, confronted as they are with a history of suffering, they themselves are made responsible and are called to account. Theodicy, the justification of God, has been transformed into anthropodicy. The accusation of God becomes at once a critique of men, women, and society.

But, Schillebeeckx asks, does this solve the problem? Has anything really changed? The defense or the accusation of God and of human persons conceals a subtle technique of self-absolution and the search for an alibi. The former alibi was God. He was the One upon whom final responsibility could be thrust. Today the Evil Doer must be sought elsewhere. What could previously be considered a matter of "foreign affairs," that is to say, a dispute between human beings and their God, has now become a matter of "internal affairs," an inner-worldly dispute among ourselves. An immanent scapegoat replaces the transcendental one.

> Thus, there develops a conflict between, on the one hand, those men who have made the world and its history into what they now painfully are, and, on the other hand, those men (and this is always ourselves) who want to make a better world and accuse 'the

[6] Schillebeeckx, "The Mystery of Injustice," 6-9.

others' of having made our world into a history of suffer Where suffering and evil manifest themselves, the one who is branded as guilty is man, but man in the form of the other, enemy, the non-ego or the not-us. The tactics of excuse and ever-returning alibi are quite clear.[7]

For Schillebeeckx, the shift from the accusation of God to accusation of humankind does not constitute a better solution

> Other people can not always be held responsible (for our hist suffering), nor even are social structures always at fault. To these latter responsible for all suffering and evil is a modern, form of the old Manichaean dualism. The responsibility of and of the structures they bring into existence, is real, even s but limited.[8]

From the Theory to a Praxis of Resistance?

In addition to the reaction against theodicy just discussed is a trend which proposes a radical halt to all kinds of expla of suffering. To theorize about suffering is a useless, if not ful, occupation. Here we meet Immanuel Kant (1724-180 rejects the idea of God's "permissive will" (because it nally contradictory: God cannot be forced to permit somet the basis of a necessary fatality) and protests against the larly pretentious character of a philosophy which profess capable of analyzing God. The result of such an adventure icature of the true God and a devaluation of human bei God of Leibniz is unrecognizable to suffering people. Th longer a holy and merciful God, in whom suffering hu trust, and to whom they can address their hope for assist forgiveness. It is not surprising that Kant rejects the red suffering humans to means at the service of a greater Totality. One of his basic principles is: "Never use a hu

[7] Ibid., 8.
[8] Ibid., 9.
[9] Immanuel Kant, *On the Failure of All Attempted Philosophica* (1791), in Michel Despland, *Kant on History and Religion* (Montreal McGill - Queen's University Press, 1973) 283-297.

of meaning consists of solidarity with the suffering and of radical resistance, whereby, in and through actual practice, one denies to suffering any right to exist. That is to say, one takes the part of good, and refuses to treat evil on the same footing as the good.[13]

Nevertheless, Schillebeeckx asks, can such a task be brought to a successful conclusion?

> Every human praxis of resistance to evil is always, at least in its pretension of totality, itself subject to critique .... On the level of our plans for an earthly human future, we are, at the same time, confronted with the final fiasco of our praxis of resistance to evil. Death, in particular, points out that it is illusory to expect, here on earth, real, perfect and universal salvation for one and all. Clearly, salvation for humankind is only salvation if it is universal and complete. As long as, alongside our personally experienced happiness, there is still suffering, oppression, and unhappiness in our immediate or more distant neighborhood, and as long as our happiness is paid for by the pain of others (and this is clearly the reality which is presented to us, for example, in the Third World), then there is no question of true salvation. Even the salvation which we wish for ourselves and others, and which we even attain in splendid fragments, is suspect because of our own final untrustworthiness. For what are our credentials for unconditional trustworthy fellowship? Is this pretention of fellowship a basis for a solid expectation? I am afraid that history will give here a skeptical answer![14]

Searching for Inspiration in the Struggle Against Evil

Theories do not suffice; our praxis is fragmentary; and we shall not be able to build a paradise on earth. The questions which suffering asks are too penetrating. They concern not only our own reliability but the endlessness of the task (only universal and complete salvation is salvation). And all of this finds place in the shadow of death. What shall we do? Where can we find the strength and the inspiration for such a praxis? Where can we find the hope to continue despite everything?

---

[13] Schillebeeckx, "The Mystery of Injustice," 11.
[14] Ibid., 12.

These are precisely the questions which incite us to continue our search for meaning. By this we do not mean an encompassing explanation à la Leibniz which justifies the status quo. We are looking for an inspirational meaning which provides the energy needed to change things. To offer some such meaning to suffering people would be an element in an effective struggle against suffering. It would assist the poor to discover at least a relative meaning in their paradoxical situation, and, as such, contribute to their struggle for human survival.

In this context, it seems harmful to dissociate theory from praxis. If one attends only to the theoretical attribution of meaning, in the fashion of Leibniz and Hegel, there is the danger that one will lose all feeling with the concrete reality. If, on the other hand, one attends only to specific instances of suffering, there is a danger one will lose oneself in praxis. Then, disappointment and despair are a continual threat. One can lose all sense of the foundation of all life and praxis.

Faithful dedication is only possible on the basis of a more encompassing perspective, a sense of meaning which transcends concrete cases but, nevertheless, inspires us to act here and now. This is the object of our quest for an inspirational meaning. It seems likely that contemporary men and women are more in need of inspiration than of explanation.

This inspirational attribution of meaning must tell us something about life's ultimate horizon, and about what lies beyond it, since, of course, it is ultimately death — our death and the death of those to whom we are dedicated — which menaces every commitment. From the point of view of the New Testament, this inspirational attribution of meaning must make reference to the general principles of the Sermon on the Mount, but also to the details of concrete service — the single cup of cold water, the only thing necessary. Inspiration — as we understand it — involves the courage to persist in the face of the divide between the theoretical attribution of meaning and concrete praxis, between the ideal and the concrete situation, between encompassing principles and the one thing necessary today.

In *After Ten Years: A Reckoning Made at New Year 1943*, Dietrich Bonhöffer (1906-1945), a Lutheran minister executed by the Gestapo, expresses the view we have been trying to develop. He concludes as follows:

> Who stands fast? Only the man whose final standard is not reason, his principles, his conscience, his freedom, or his virtue, but who is ready to sacrifice all this when he is called to obedient and responsible action in faith and in exclusive allegiance to God — the responsible man, who tries to make his whole life an answer to the question and call of God. Where are these responsible people?[15]

Significance, a Service to the Sufferers

Gisbert Greshake provides additional reasons for engaging in the quest for inspirational meaning. He, too, rejects the dichotomy between experience and theory. This rejection was inspired, first of all, by the fact that his own most intense reflection upon suffering came shortly after he had passed through a dangerous illness. Moreover, it was his experience that it is the whole person, and not simply the intellect, who engages in the quest for meaning.

> [The question of the Why of suffering] conceals or abbreviates the urgent question: 'How can I overcome suffering, so as to integrate it into my life?' For the believer it also includes: 'How can I abandon myself without reserve, and cling to God in faith, without letting my situation lead me to despair of His goodness and power?' And such urgent questioning is anything but mere theory, nor can it be satisfied with an automatic conclusion drawn from a consistent doctrine.[16]

It is obvious, Greshake adds, that no theory about suffering can solve the anguished question arising from personal pain. On the other hand, however, realistic theology is obliged to ask along what lines suffering should be understood so that it can be exis-

---

[15] Dietrich Bonhoeffer, *After Ten Years: A Reckoning Made at New Year 1943*, in *Letters and Papers from Prison* (London: SCM, 1973) 4-5, p.5.

[16] Gisbert Greshake, "Suffering and the Question of God," *Stauros-Bulletin*, no. 1 (1977) 4.

tentially integrated. No theory of suffering, by itself, is an ade-
quate solution. It can, however, provide the framework within
which a solution is to be sought.[17]

For this to take place, however, two conditions must be fulfilled.
First of all, the offer of an authentic framework for meaning must
include a long period of silent listening and closeness. This is what
Job's friends teach us, in spite of their shortcomings: "And his
friends sat with him on the ground seven days and seven nights,
and no one spoke a word to him, for they saw that his suffering was
very great." Seven days and seven nights — the time needed for
creation.[18] Secondly, it seems that the best way to offer such a
framework will probably be by means of the narrative genre. The
story of an experience of meaning born of a struggle (not of mere
triumph) can function as an example. This can serve as an invitation to look for links between one's own life-story — in all its par-
ticularity — and the experiences of other people. Through the ages,
this has been the function of the stories of the saint's lives, and, in
this sense, they are more important than theodicies.

The final reason to continue our search for meaning is the fact
that many people lose their faith in the struggle with suffering,
though it is also a fact that other people (re-) discover faith in and
through this confrontation. How is this possible? Is it because the
latter engage a different God or have a different view of His
power? This problem demands clarification. Hence, we go on asking the question of the meaning of so much suffering, without,
however, forgetting that the ultimate aim of such questioning is
the cause of those who actually do suffer. Harold Kushner offers a
good example of the way in which the attribution of meaning
arises out of an intensely existential experience of suffering.

---

[17] Ibid., 7.
[18] Job 2:13. W.R. van der Zee, *Wie heeft daar woorden voor? Een pastorale over
lijdende mensen en een leidende God* ('s Gravenhage: Boekencentrum, 1981) 12
and Herman Wiersinga, *Verzoening met het lijden?* (Baarn: Ten Have, 1975) 8
recall the Jewish custom which forbids "verbal" consolation before the burial.
The mourning person should not be left alone - not even for a while - but the visitors should not try to console with words. Grief must have free play. This is real
con-dolence, suffering-together-with.

2. GOD IS LOVE — WHAT ABOUT HIS POWER?

Harold S. Kushner (°1935) is a rabbi of Temple Israel in Nat-ick, Massachusetts, U.S.A. He was personally confronted with suffering when he was informed about the illness of his three-year-old son, Aaron. Aaron suffered from progeria, rapid aging. Aaron died at the age of fourteen. Out of this experience Harold Kushner wrote *When Bad Things Happen to Good People* in 1981[19].

Harold Kushner and Job

Kushner starts from the Book of Job, since Job helps him to formulate the dilemma with which his son's suffering confronted him. He expresses the central theses as follows: (A) God is all-powerful and causes everything that happens in the world. Nothing happens without His willing it. (B) God is just and fair, and stands for people getting what they deserve so that good people prosper and the wicked are punished. (C) Job is a good person.[20]

There are very few problems with this reasoning as long as everything goes well. But as soon as one is confronted with suf-fering, the internal cohesion of the three propositions becomes questionable. One can no longer make sense of all three statements together, for one can now affirm any two only by denying the third. This is done in the Book of Job.

Job's friends are prepared to stop believing in proposition C: Job is not a good person. Either he keeps up appearances or he is unaware of his guilt. Their intervention aims at an examination of Job's conscience.

[19] All references to Kushner will be to the third edition (New York: Avon Books, 1983).
[20] Ibid., 37.

Job is inclined to reject proposition B. In his self-defense and in the purification oath he claims his innocence. Job calls God "a watcher of men" (7:20); "The almighty has terrified me" (23:16); even more explicitly, he claims, "God has put me in the wrong" (19:6). According to Kushner, God appears in the Book of Job as an Oriental potentate, with unchallenged power over the life and property of his subjects. Why should He permit Satan to test Job in such a terrible way (1:12; 2:6)? Moreover, God's answer at the end of the story is pretentious, and deliberately beside the question (38-41). And is everything resolved when Job's possessions are returned (42:10-17)? What about the pain endured? No, the God Job meets "is so powerful that He does not need to be fair."[21]

Kushner suggests that the author of the Book of Job takes the position which neither Job nor his friends take. He believes in God's goodness and in Job's goodness, and is prepared to give up his belief in proposition A: that God is all-powerful. "Bad things do happen to good people in this world, but it is not God who wills it. God would like people to get what they deserve in this life, but He cannot always arrange it. Forced to choose between a good God who is not totally powerful, or a powerful God who is not totally good, the author of the Book of Job chooses to believe in God's goodness."[22]

In order to found his thesis on exegetical grounds, Kushner proposes a very uncommon interpretation of the theophany in Job. In opposition to the traditional reading that understands the theophany as God's intervention to demonstrate that He holds the whole world in His hands (even Leviathan, symbol of the primordial chaos), Kushner inverts the meaning of these verses. According to him, they mean that it is not easy for God to keep the world straight and true, and to keep unfair things from happening to people. Consequently, people should not be astonished if God does not manage to give them what they deserve. So, in Kushner's

---

[21] Ibid., 43.
[22] Ibid., 42-43.

view, God asks Job, "If you have a stronger arm, and think you would be able to do things better than I do, please, try it." It is within this framework that Kushner formulates his main thesis.

God is not All-Powerful

> Innocent people do suffer misfortunes in this life.... When it happens, it does not represent God punishing them for something they did wrong. The misfortunes do not come from God at all. There may be a sense of loss at coming to this conclusion. In a way, it was comforting to believe in an all-wise, all-powerful God who guaranteed fair treatment and happy endings, who reassured us that everything happened for a reason .... But it was comforting the way the religion of Job's friends was comforting: it worked only as long as we did not take the problems of innocent victims seriously. When we have met Job, when we have *been* Job, we cannot believe in that sort of God any longer without giving up our own right to feel angry, to feel that we have been treated badly by life. From that perspective, there ought to be a sense of relief in coming to the conclusion that God is not doing this to us. If God is a God of justice, and not of power, then He can still be on our side when bad things happen to us. He can know that we are good and honest people who deserve better. Our misfortunes are none of His doing, and so we can turn to Him for help. Our question will not be Job's question, 'God, why are You doing this to me?' but rather 'God, see what is happening to me. Can You help me?' We will turn to God, not to be judged or forgiven, not to be rewarded or punished, but to be strengthened and comforted.[23]

According to Kushner, many existential benefits are connected with the abandonment of the idea of an all-powerful God. For example, people no longer hold on to unrealistic expectations of God and, consequently, are not disappointed when these are not realized. This is a good thing because one who is angry at God loses the experience of His nearness. Moreover, people will not feel judged and condemned by God, if He does not provide what they ask of Him. They recognize that the fulfillment of their wishes does not depend on His judgement about whether or not we deserve this or that. In the same way, people stop condemning

---

[23] Ibid., 44.

themselves to guilt if misfortunes occur. They can be angry about
what has happened, without being angry with God. What is more,
they know that God is on their side, and is Himself angered by the
unfairness of life: "Instead of feeling that we are opposed to God,
we can feel that our indignation is God's anger at unfairness work-
ing through us, that when we cry out, we are still on God's side,
and He is still on ours."[24]

An Unfinished Creation

As soon as we say, "Misfortune does not come from God,"
another question arises, "Where does it come from?" Kushner
answers with a counterquestion: "Why can you not accept that
some things just happen for no reason, that there is randomness in
the universe?" Sometimes we are able to understand "how" misfortunes happen (for example, a forest fire), but there is no rea-
sonable answer to "why" this particular person died in the fire, or
why this specific sperm-cell provokes trisomy 21 with this specific
egg-cell. Does God intervene when a drunken driver avoids my
car and hits my neighbor's? How could you explain this to my
neighbor's wife? We should be courageous enough, Kushner
writes, to conclude that some things thwart God's plans as well as
ours, and that we cannot find any reason for it.

As befits a rabbi, Kushner looks for arguments in the Bible. "In
the beginning" God began his creative work in the chaos, separating the light from the darkness, the earth from the sky, the dry land
from the seas. According to Kushner — and in opposition to
almost the entire Christian tradition — to create does not mean to
make something out of nothing, but to make order out of chaos.
Kushner makes a comparison with the creative activity of a scientist or a historian. They do not make up facts. They order and
organize facts. Scientists search for connections between facts
rather than seeing them as random data. This is exactly what God

did. He fashioned a world whose overriding principle was orderliness, predictability, in place of the chaos with which He started. In this manner God arranged regular sunrises, regular sunsets, regular tides, and so on.[25]

However, God did not quite finish his work by closing time on the sixth day. If we accept that creation — the process of replacing chaos with order — is still going on, we can understand that pockets of chaos remain in the midst of a world where chaos has already been replaced by cosmos. This will be particularly true with respect to human beings, who are very recent creations on the evolutionary scale. The chaos which remains is randomness. Haphazardness does not conceal a message. Randomness does not reflect God's choice. Arbitrariness is there where God's creative, ordering Spirit has not yet penetrated. In this sense, bad things do not happen in opposition the orderly laws of nature, but outside them. "It may yet come to pass that, as 'Friday afternoon' of the world's evolution ticks towards the Great Sabbath which is the End of Days, the impact of random evil will be diminished."[26] In the meantime it remains disturbing that randomness does not differentiate between good and wicked people. A bullet has no conscience; neither does a tumor.

An Unfinished Liberty

There is at least a second reason why God should not be declared guilty of suffering in the world: human freedom. Kushner cites Genesis: "Let us make Man in our image" (1:26). Human beings are "in God's image" because of their capacity to make free decisions. This is the part of human beings that lifts them above the instinctive animal level. This is why there is a Tree of the Knowledge of Good and Evil in the Garden of Eden (Gen. 3:5) for human beings and not for animals. Human beings live in a world of good and bad, and that makes their lives painful and complicated. The "image of God" in human beings permits them

---

[25] Ibid., 51-52.
[26] Ibid., 55.

to say no to instinct on moral grounds. Freedom, good, and evil are three inextricable dimensions of human existence.

> 'Behold, I have set before you the path of good and the path of evil, the way of life and the way of death. Choose Life' (Deuteronomy 30:19). That could not be said to any other living creature except Man, for no other creature is free to choose. But if Man is truly free to choose, if he can show himself as being virtuous by freely choosing the good when the bad is equally possible, then he has to be free to choose the bad also. If he were only free to do good, he would not really be choosing. If we are *bound* to do good, then we are not free to *choose* it.[27]

Human freedom includes the possibility of choosing egotistically, against one's fellow humans. God cannot intervene to keep us doing it without taking away the freedom that makes us human beings. The first chapters of Genesis tell of these conflicts. The whole history of humankind witnesses to it, right up to the Holocaust:

> Where was God while all this was going on? Why did He not intervene to stop it? Why didn't He strike Hitler dead in 1939 and spare millions of lives and untold suffering, or why didn't He send an earthquake to demolish the gas chambers? Where was God? I have to believe, with Dorothee Sölle, that He was with the victims, and not with the murderers, but that He does not control man's choosing between good and evil. I have to believe that the tears and prayers of the victims aroused God's compassion, but having given Man freedom to choose, including the freedom to choose to hurt his neighbor, there was nothing God could do to prevent it.[28]

Nevertheless, if we acquit God of guilt in this way, another danger arises: namely, that human beings continuously blame themselves. Self-criticism is sometimes true and valuable. Indeed, human beings do provoke evil. Feelings of guilt are certainly not always misplaced. But there are also many unwarranted feelings of guilt, of the type expressed in such remarks as, "If only I had tried this or that, maybe my husband would not have died."

[27] Ibid., 79.
[28] Ibid., 84-85.

As far as this sort of guilt is concerned, Kushner repeats the same basic principles. In the first place, why is there this strenuous need to seek a cause and a reason for everything that happens? In the second place, why should we be the cause of what happens, especially when bad things happen? This excessive sense of guilt, of blaming ourselves for things which are clearly not our fault, robs us of our self-esteem and of our capacity to grow. We simply have to accept that there is still chaos in the universe, and that amidst this chaos the orderly laws of cause and effect do not exist. Otherwise it would not be chaos. The fact that, on occasion, the cause of a particular accident can be designated, does not mean it could have been prevented. God does not have everything under control and neither do human beings. There is still chaos in the universe, and in human freedom too. However, human megalomania makes it difficult to accept this.

The Meanings of Prayers

If one no longer holds God responsible for life's tragedies, if one believes that He wants justice but cannot always arrange it, what can be the meaning of prayer? Is God still capable of intervening in order to effect the favorable resolution of a crisis?

Yes, Kushner answers, it is essential for a believer to pray; but it is equally essential to change people's current understanding of what it means to pray, and what it means for prayers to be answered. Bad prayers ask for things God cannot give. Bad prayers, which cannot be answered, provoke anger with God and diminish His nearness. A pregnant woman should not ask to have a girl or a boy. Upon hearing the fire alarm, people should not pray, "Please God, don't let the fire be in my house" (because this prayer means: "Let the fire be in someone else's house instead of mine"). It is unacceptable to ask God to change the laws of nature for personal benefit or to effect specific miracles. Sometimes miracles do happen. On such occasions people should be grateful. They should not, however, think that their prayers provoked it. The next time they try and there is no miracle, they may wonder why their prayers are ineffective. This breeds disappointment or, when others are the beneficiaries, even jealousy. The worst prayers of all are those which are intended to harm others.[29]

However, if we cannot pray for the impossible or the unnatural, and if we cannot pray for vengeance, what is there left to pray for? What can prayer do to help when people are hurt? Praying does two things, Kushner answers. It puts people in touch with other people, and it puts people in touch with God.

Prayers put people in touch with other people who share the same concerns, joys, and pains regarding the mysteries of growth, love, birth, suffering, and death. To pray means not to leave each other alone. This is a basic purpose of religion: to help people not to have to face the most joyous and frightening moments of life alone. This is especially the case as regards the most frightening moments, those moments when people feel singled out by the hand of fate, when they are tempted to crawl off into a dark corner and feel sorry for themselves. Religion reminds them of the fact that they are surrounded by other people who care about them, and that they are still part of the stream of life. "I will pray for your recovery" means at least, "I feel with you, I share in your pain, I care about you."

Kushner provides a humorous example: "Harry Golden tells that when he was young, he once asked his father, 'If you don't believe in God, why do you go to synagogue?' His father answered, 'Jews go to synagogue for all sorts of reasons. My friend Garfinkle who is Orthodox, goes to talk to God. I go to talk to Garfinkle.'"[30]

---

[29] Kushner tells the story of two shopkeepers who were bitter rivals. Their stores were across the street from each other, and they would spend each day sitting in the doorway, keeping track of each other's business. One night, an angel appeared to one of the shopkeepers and said, "God has sent me to teach you a lesson. He will give you anything you ask for, but I want you to know that, whatever you get, your competitor across the street will get twice as much." The man frowned, thought for a moment, and said, "All right, my request is: strike me blind in one eye." See Kushner, *When Bad Things Happen to Good People*, 117.

[30] Ibid., 122.

Beside their communal function, prayers put us in touch with God, except, of course, when people ask Him to effect the impossible. On such occasions, prayers have the contrary effect, especially if things do not turn out as one had wished.

True prayer, however, is a gradual process. Initially, prayers often are "mercantile": benefit for benefit, like the first prayer of the young Jacob, fleeing from God and promising everything on the condition that God answers his demands: "Then Jacob made a vow, saying, 'If God will be with me, and will keep me in this way that I go, and will give me bread to eat and clothing to wear, so that I come again to my father's house in peace, then the Lord shall be my God, and this stone, which I have set up for a pillar, shall be God's house; and of all that you givest me I will give the tenth to thee.'" (Genesis 28:20-22)

At the same river bank, but twenty years later, Jacob prays again. He is once again anxious and afraid, but he no longer tries to make a deal with God. He no longer bargains. He only asks God to be on his side so that whatever the future may bring, he will not have to face it alone: "O God of my father Abraham and God of my father Isaac, I am not worthy of the least of all the steadfast love and all the faithfulness which thou hast shown to thy servant, for with only my staff I crossed the Jordan; and now I have become two companies. Deliver me, I pray thee, from the hand of my brother Esau, for I fear him, lest he come and slay us all, the mothers with the children. But thou didst say, 'I will do you good, and make your descendants as the sand of thee sea, which cannot be numbered for multitude.'" (Genesis 32:9-12)

This kind of prayer is answered, Kushner asserts.

> People who pray for courage, for strength to bear the unbearable, for the grace to remember what they have left instead of what they have lost, very often find their prayers answered .... Their prayers helped them tap hidden reserves of faith and courage which were not available to them before .... I would like to believe that they received those things from the context of a concerned community, people who made it clear to them that they cared, and from the knowledge that God is at the side of the afflicted and the downcast ....

We don't have to beg or bribe God to give us strength or hope or
patience. We need only turn to Him, admit that we can't do this on
our own, and understand that bravely bearing up under long-term
illness is one of the most human, and one of the most godly, things
we can ever do. One of the things that constantly reassures me that
God is real, and not just an idea that religious leaders made up, is
the fact that people who pray for strength, hope, and courage so
often find resources of strength, hope, and courage that they did
not have before they prayed.[31]

Kushner illustrates with an example about a widow who prayed
that her husband would not die of cancer. He died. "My prayer did
not have any result." "It had," Kushner answers, "You didn't get
a miracle to avert a tragedy. But you discovered people around
you, and God beside you, and strength within you to help you survive the tragedy. I offer that as an example of a prayer being
answered."[32]

A Humble Meaning for Suffering

At the end of his book, Kushner seeks to formulate a new, humble meaning for suffering, because what is completely meaningless, is unbearable. To give up making God responsible for suffering does not imply that suffering is simply meaningless.
Nevertheless, not God, but human beings must give a meaning to
suffering:

Let me suggest that the bad things that happen to us in our lives do
not have a meaning when they happen to us. They do not happen
for any good reason which would cause us to accept them will-
ingly. But we can give them a meaning. We can redeem these
tragedies from senselessness by imposing meaning on them. The
question we should be asking is not, 'Why did this happen to me?'
What did I do to deserve this?' This is really an unanswerable,
pointless question. A better question would be 'Now that this has
happened to me, what am I going to do about it?'[33]

[31] Ibid., 125, 128.
[32] Ibid., 131.
[33] Ibid., 136.

As a good example of the active attribution of meaning to senseless suffering Kushner refers to Martin Gray who survived the Warsaw Ghetto and the Holocaust, lost his family in a forest fire, and wrote a book, *For Those I Loved*. After the forest fire people urged him to demand an inquiry. But, instead, Gray chose to put his resources into a movement to protect nature from future fires. An inquiry would focus only on the past and set him against others, those accused of being responsible for the tragedy. All of this only makes a lonely person lonelier. Life, he concluded, has to be lived for something, not just against something.[34]

This can be expressed positively by saying that the only meaning of life is love. Love is challenged by suffering and suffering challenges love. Kushner quotes Archibald MacLeish:

> Man depends on God for all things; God depends on man for one. Without Man's love, God does not exist as God, only as creator, and love is the one thing no one, not even God Himself, can command. It is a free gift, or it is nothing. And it is most itself, most free, when it is offered in spite of suffering, of injustice, and of death.[35]

Finally, Kushner summarizes his search for a meaning by providing a sketch of his image of God:

> We do not love God because He is perfect. We do not love Him because He protects us from all harm and keeps evil things from happening to us. We do not love Him because we are afraid of Him, or because He will hurt us if we turn our back on Him. We love Him because He is God, because He is the author of all the beauty and the order around us, the source of our strength and the hope and courage within us, and of other people's strength and hope and courage with which we are helped in our time of need. We love Him because He is the best part of ourselves and of our world. That is what it means to love. Love is not the admiration of perfection, but the acceptance of an imperfect person with all his imperfections.[36]

---

[34] Ibid., 136-137.
[35] Ibid., 146.
[36] Ibid., 146-147.

Is this Kushner's answer to the question of why bad things happen to good people? According to Kushner, everything depends on what is meant by "answer". There is no explanation which will make sense of it all. After all the learned explanations have been proffered, the pain and the sense of unfairness will remain. However, if "answer" means "response," there may well be a satisfactory answer to the tragedies which mark human lives:

> In the final analysis, the question of why bad things happen to good people translates itself into some very different questions, no longer asking why something happened, but asking how we will respond, what we intend to do now that it has happened.
>
> Are you capable of forgiving and accepting in love a world which has disappointed you by not being perfect, a world in which there is so much unfairness and cruelty, disease and crime, earthquake and accident? Can you forgive its imperfections, and love it because it is capable of containing great beauty and goodness, and because it is the only world we have?
>
> Are you capable of forgiving and loving the people around you, even if they have hurt you and let you down by not being perfect? Can you forgive them and love them, because there aren't any perfect people around, and because the penalty for not being able to love imperfect people is condemning oneself to loneliness?
>
> Are you capable of forgiving and loving God even when you have found out that He is not perfect, even when He has let you down and disappointed you by permitting bad luck and sickness and cruelty in His world, and permitting some of those things to happen to you? Can you learn to love and forgive Him despite His limitations, as Job does, and as you once learned to forgive and love your parents even though they were not as wise, as strong, or as perfect as you needed them to be?
>
> And if you can do these things, will you be able to recognize that the ability to forgive and the ability to love are the weapons God has given us to enable us to live fully, bravely, and meaningfully in this less-than-perfect world?[37]

[37] Ibid., 147-148.

3. THE (IM)POTENCY OF LOVE

In the previous section we developed two contrasting views of suffering. We began by discussing classic theodicy, under the heading, "God is all-powerful, what about His love?" There we encountered the image of an almighty God who controls everything and "knows what is best." We cannot help but feel that while the theory may be theoretically convincing, suffering people are left out in the cold. God is all-powerful, but distant. We then moved on to consider an alternate image of God, under the heading, "God is love — what about his power?" Here, there is a real place for suffering people. God is near and loving. But, does He still have things under control? God is present, but powerless, Huub Oosterhuis writes:[38]

> Impossible god, god with a nothing name,
> little god who cannot cope
> with people,
> with their gods of money and violence.
> God of Jesus.
> To Him will always happen,
> what happened
> to this powerless man of Nazareth.
> He follows the path of all seed.
> He is always the least among men and women.
> All poverty is God's poverty.
> All that is insignificant and humiliated
> brings Him to mind.
> To believe, to pray, means
> to endure with the God of Jesus
> or
> to share in God's suffering,
> to share in God's impotence
> in this world.

A Conversion to Reality

The inversion of perspectives that finds place as we move between the two views of suffering already discussed is salutary.

---

[38] Huub Oosterhuis, *In het voorbijgaan* (Utrecht: Ambo, 1968) 20-21.

The shift from the all-powerful to the all-loving God involves the transition from over-confidence to humility. This is an essential trajectory on the way to a faith-filled existence.[39] To be humble means to be open to the questions raised by reality. The Lisbon earthquake prompted Voltaire and Kant to protest against Leibniz. Kushner's reflections are colored by the death of his son. In our day, reflection on suffering and on God cannot avoid the dreadful reality of Auschwitz.

To allow ourselves to be questioned by reality is more than a formal decision. It has consequences for the content of our reflection. This way of thinking includes a sort of (Freudian) conversion to reality. This means that reflection no longer starts from a world "that could have been," but from reality "as it is." We can and should long for the end of all suffering, but we gain nothing by denying reality.

If we reflect on the amazing complexity of the development of a human being in the womb, and of the functioning of the human body, we can only wonder at the fact that these processes are so often unimpaired. Even the most superficial psychology is compelled to acknowledge that the human person is a mixture of instinct and spirit, that the capacity to love is matched by the capacity to hate, that human sexuality can be destructive. Could God have created a free human being, moved by passions, who would never practice injustice, cruelty or violence? It is not insignificant that the first chapters of the Bible recount the deeds of sinful human beings, and that one of the first human crimes was fratricide.

The concern for reality in all its concreteness is evident in so-called "process-theology."[40] Process-thinking underlines the self-

---

[39] Walter Kasper, "Anthropologische Aspekte der Busse," *Theologische Quartalschrift* 163 (1983) 104.

[40] See, for example, John B. Cobb, *God and the World* (Philadelphia: Westminster, 1969) 87-102; Nancy Frankenberry, "Some Problems in Process Theodicy," *Religious Studies* 17 (1981) 179-197; Charles Hartshorne, *Omnipotence and Other Theological Mistakes* (Albany, NY: State University of New York Press, 1984); Jan Van der Veken, *God and Change: Process Thought and the Christian*

activity of all that exists. It leaves room for contingency, randomness, and coincidence. The Universe is not the result of one Will
which decides upon everything. Concrete reality consists of the
combined action of billions of entities. Each element seeks to realize itself. No element is possessed of an overview of the whole.
Consequently, it is not astonishing that there are conflicts. On the
contrary, it is wondrous that, in the face of such multiplicity, there
is still one world. From this perspective, evil is unavoidable: it
arises from the conflicts between entities intent on their own self-
realization.

Conflicting feelings cause pain and tension. Cancer-cells are
experienced as evil because they literally do not stay put, but
spread throughout the body. From the amoral standpoint of the
cancer-cells, however, it is a struggle for life. A volcano does not
reckon with the people who choose to cultivate its fertile slopes.
You cannot blame a volcano.

Kushner's vision assists the process of conversion to reality,
and to the abandonment of illusory dreams about what the world
might have been. It is one of the merits of his work. Moreover, his
reflections contribute to a more "realistic" or unpretentious view
of God. This was Job's experience. Job stops telling God how He
should be. He is converted. He turns to the real God, by abandon-
ing those fantasies of omnipotence, which he had projected onto
God.

Human beings spontaneously fill in the concept of God with
their own dreams. This is the risk involved in all analogical thinking about God. Starting from the most eminent human experiences, one concludes: God should be like that or even better. The
confrontation with suffering, however, can bring the whole rational edifice tumbling down. Then, people often reject God instead
of their own ideas about Him.

The process of giving a concrete meaning to God is a risky
undertaking, but can it be avoided? The word "God" is an empty

Doctrine of God (Leuven: Center for Metaphysics and Philosophy of God, 1987);
Johan Vanhoutte, "God as Companion and Fellow-sufferer: An Image Emerging
from Process Thought," *Archivio di Filosofia* 56 (1988) 191-225.

concept or a mere theoretical principle unless it is connected to daily life. Nevertheless if God is really God, then He differs from our spontaneous longings and representations, which are based on human experiences of caring love. The Bible, too, applies terms such as goodness, justice and caring providence to God but, again and again, these concepts are invalidated by contrasting images in order to disrupt spontaneous thought about God, thought which is simply the extension of human experience.

This filling-in of concepts of God finds place on the subjective-psychological level as well as on the theological level. For centuries, theology has, so to speak, confronted God with the dilemma provoked by the attempt to reconcile the categories 'all-powerful' and 'all-good'. The presupposition behind this dilemma is that God could have created a world different from this one. We can, indeed, long for a different world, but we cannot, in fact, conclude that this other world is either possible or impossible. We simply do not know any other world. Certainly, it is possible to vaguely imagine a totally different creation. As soon, however, as we try to give some intelligible content to that idea, we realize that it is nothing more than a phantasm, a redesigned version of our world, albeit devoid of this world's defects. In short, we project an absurdity. Our insights are limited because our judgments, even in their theoretical conceptualization, depend on our perceptions of the given world.

A Conversion to the Otherness of God

Kushner's realistic view of the world and his concern to reckon with life's realities are praiseworthy. One may, however, ask if he has taken sufficient account of the otherness of God. Kushner does not leave behind the classic dilemma between power and love. He simply turns it upside down. He continues to deploy one concept at the expense of the other. Classic theodicy stresses God's omnipotence, and is prepared to sacrifice His goodness. Kushner reflects on God's goodness at the expense of His omnipotence. He does not manage to connect the two concepts. He cannot do so because, to his mind, power remains power. He reflects on power, starting from disappointing human experiences with (the abuse of) power. For this reason, he rejects every allusion to God's power[41] but, at the same time, every possibility of divine intervention in human history. A divine intervention that does not contradict human freedom is inconceivable for Kushner, although the Old Testament frequently attests to such interventions. The consequence of this option is that human beings must themselves give meaning to suffering. In a sense, they themselves must make up what God cannot supply.

But what remains of God's love when it has been purged of every notion of power? The answer would appear to be, nothing but a sentimental and perfectly inefficacious image.[42] Because the concept of "power" is not "converted" in Kushner's theology, he is unable to pray for effective deliverance from suffering. However, both the Scriptures and the Christian faith tradition confirm God's omnipotence and His caring providence. In Christian faith, the qualification, "the Almighty," is as essential to the notion of God as the qualification, "the Loving One." Consequently, it is legitimate to inquire whether the power of evil is met by the power of God. To ask the question of what it means to be "saved by God's omnipotence" is not a sign of bad faith. Is there a real link between God and the victory over death, between God and the reign of freedom? Which power do we believe the good God has over evil? Where and how is His power over evil at work? All these questions are legitimate, especially in the face of the continuing power of evil. The ultimate reason for reexamining the question of God's power is the reality of hope.

One might ask whether the humility which Kushner and others rightly advocate does not issue in resignation. In fact, there is no need to posit a dilemma between arrogant overconfidence and timid pusillanimity. True humility exists somewhere between

---

[41] Douglas John Hall, *God and Human Suffering: An Exercise in the Theology of the Cross* (Minneapolis: Augsburg Publishing House, 1986) 156-157.

[42] Stanley Hauerwas, *Naming the Silences: God, Medicine, and the Problem of Evil* (Grand Rapids: Eerdmans, 1990) 56.

these extremes and is possessed of magnanimity, the courage of great things made real in little things.

Vergote puts the problem very well:

> We can no longer conceive of God's goodness and omnipotence in terms of the naively-arrogant and contradictory representations of our desire. To confess God's omnipotence has a religious sense. It means to recognize that God is the absolute origin, the Lord of the cosmos and of history. To attribute omnipotence to God means to recognize that He is the personal, creative, and lifegiving force of which the universe, life and love are signs .... To confess God's omnipotence does not mean that we are able to make a representation of God's power in itself ....
>
> To confess God's goodness also has a religious meaning. This confession consists of the remembrance of the goodness of creation as a divine gift. For human beings this world is a place where, in spite of suffering, they can find a limited happiness in enjoying the beauty of nature, in the exploration of the secrets of the world, in the creativity of a civilization, in giving and receiving human love, in discovering God's manifestation in this earthly goodness. For those who make unlimited demands, life will be mostly suffering, and the words 'God's goodness' will make no sense. Those persons, on the contrary, who limit their demands and are tolerant of suffering, who accept life as a task and the situation as a challenge, will attend to the good things, and thank God while confessing his goodness, in spite of and in the midst of disappointed expectations, and against the desire to call God to account.[43]

Hosea: Powerless Love

If we attempt to combine the concepts of power and of love and to discover something like a power of love, the first thing we encounter is the weakness and the impotence of love. It is only through this purifying experience that the specific power of love is manifest.

In the Bible God appears as a loving God. This image is present from the beginning, but its distinctive features are progressively revealed throughout the course of the Old Testament. Gradually

---

[43] Antoon Vergote, *Het meerstemmige leven: Gedachten over mens en religie* (Kapellen: Pelckmans, 1987) 77-78.

the people of Israel became aware that their God wanted to enter into a personal relationship with each of them and with the people as a whole, the Covenant.

The consciousness of evil evolves within this framework. Initially, there was a primitive fear of the forces of revenge, forces which could be quasi automatically unleashed by any human failing, even those for which the person was not directly responsible. Later on, this experience developed into a specific awareness of sin. There is sin where a human being — consciously and freely — damages or breaks an alliance of love. Sin is a concept that belongs to the sphere of the Covenant.[44]

The experience of a loving God and, consequently, of sin as a violation of love, is very strong in prophetic preaching. It reaches a summit in Hosea's "ballads of a unrequited love."[45] Hosea's prophecy is a last warning to his people: "Turn back to your Lord. Without the religious dimension, there is no human society. If you abandon the Lord, idols will replace Him." Isaiah called this fundamental sin pride. Hosea calls it adultery. Hosea is not afraid to resort to provocative terms: *Osée est parfois osé*.

God asks the prophet Hosea to be a living symbol of His adulterous people. This shocking symbolization is intended to awaken His people.

> The Lord said to Hosea, 'Go, take to yourself a wife of harlotry and have children of harlotry, for the land commits great harlotry by forsaking the Lord.' So he went and took Gomer, and she conceived and bore him a son.
> And the Lord said to him, 'Call his name Jezreel - God Will Sow; for yet a little while, and I will punish the house of Jehu for the blood of Jezreel.'
> She conceived again and bore a daughter. And the Lord said to him, 'Call her name Lo-Ruchama — Not Pitied —, for I will no more have pity on the house of Israel.'

[44] Ricoeur, *The Symbolism of Evil*, 25-99.
[45] The expression comes from Hendrik Van Den Bussche, "De ballade der miskende liefde," *Collationes Brugenses et Gandavenses* 4 (1958) 434-466.

> When she had weaned Not Pitied, she conceived and bore a son.
> And the Lord said, 'Call his name Lo-Ammi — Not My People —,
> for you are not my people and I am not your God.' (1:2-9)

On a first level of interpretation of this symbolic story, the
prophet is willy-nilly married to his people. Now he has to tell them
the truth: people commit evil and confer upon it a sacred color.
They worship the Lord, but only formally, and, in the meantime,
they run after other gods. This is exactly what temple prostitutes like
Gomer do. On a second level of interpretation, Hosea symbolizes
God. God is married to a people who prostitutes itself. To engage in
evil is not without consequences. The first consequence of adultery
is called Jezreel, etymologically "to sow calamity" or "disperse."
But Jezreel is also the name of a plain, where the leader of the opposition, the later King Jehu, had murdered his predecessor, King
Joram, with his staff. Jezreel is a place of shame. In contemporary
terms, we would say: "Call your child Auschwitz or Sarajevo." The
second consequence of evil is "Pitilessness." Every kind of solidarity among people disappears. The third consequence of evil (or
unfaithfulness) is God's change of His own name. Formerly, He had
been called "I-will-be-your-God." From now on, His name will be,
"I am no longer your God."

Even the birth of the children-of-evil does not change anything.
God becomes angry. His anger is the anger of painful love, of
powerless love. Hosea (*cum quo* God) will reject his wife. Nevertheless, behind even these cruel threats, there is nostalgia and ten-
derness:

> Plead with your mother, plead — for she is not my wife, and I am
> not her husband — that she put away her harlotry from her face, and
> her adultery from between her breasts; lest I strip her naked and
> make her as in the day she was born, and make her like a wilderness,
> and set her like a parched land, and slay her with thirst .... For she
> said, 'I will go after my lovers, who give me my bread and my
> water, my wool and my flax, my oil and my drink.' Therefore I will
> hedge up her way with thorns; and I will build a wall against her, so
> that she cannot find her paths. Then she shall say, 'I will go and
> return to my first husband, for it was better with me then than now.'
> (2:2-3,5-7)

This is the first series of measures to bring Gomer back home. Maybe she will be converted, even if only out of egoistic motives. It fails, however, and stronger measures must be taken. Hosea (God) explodes with rage. But, all of a sudden, the story breaks down. It is as if God suddenly realizes that the destruction of His people would be in flagrant contradiction with His own divine essence. Perhaps the only outcome is to love still more ....

> I will punish her for the feast days of the Baals when she burned incense to them and decked herself with her ring and jewelry, and went after her lovers, and forgot me, says the Lord.
> Therefore behold, I will allure her, and bring her into the wilderness, and speak tenderly to her. (2:13-14)

In the Bible the symbol of the desert is possessed of a double meaning: on the one hand, it is void and empty, it suggests isolation and desolation; on the other hand — perhaps in view of the first sense — it is a place where a romance can start or start again. In the desert, devoid of all their defense mechanisms, people are once again able to hear the voice of the heart. So God hopes. The Valley of Achor, once a place of terrible defeat (Joshua 7:26), will become a door of hope. Misery will turn into joy. It will be a renewed creation, a new alliance with nature (even with reptiles) and between people. The two sources of evil — human beings and nature — will be purified. The future will be betrothal and marriage instead of harlotry and adultery. This new covenant will be based on justice (concrete measures and clear agreements) and on a deeper feeling for righteousness, on goodness and on mercy (*misericordia*), and especially on faithfulness. If this reconciliation occurs, God will adopt the children-of-evil and change their names. Even they become the signs of a love that overcomes evil.

> And there I will give her her vineyards and make the Valley of Achor a door of hope. And there she shall answer as in the days of her youth, as at the time she came out of the land of Egypt. And in that day, says the Lord, you will call me, 'My husband'.
> And I will make for you a covenant on that day with the beasts of the field, the birds of the air, and the creeping things of the

ground; and I will abolish the bow, the sword, and war from the
land; and I will make you lie down in safety. And I will betroth
you to me for ever; I will betroth you to me in righteousness and
in justice, in steadfast love, and in mercy. I will betroth you to me
in faithfulness; and you shall know the Lord. And I will sow him
for myself in the land. And I shall have pity on Not Pitied, and I
will say to Not My People, 'You are my people'; and he shall say,
'Thou art my God.'" (2:15-16,18-20,23)

Chapter 11 of the Book of Hosea deals with the relationship
between a parent and a stubborn child:

When Israel was a child, I loved him,
and out of Egypt I called my son.
The more I called them,
the more they went from me;
they kept sacrificing to the Baals,
and burning incense to idols.

Yet it was I who taught Ephraim to walk,
I took them up in my arms;
but they did not know that I healed them.
I led them with cords of compassion,
with the bands of love,
and I became to them as one
who eases the yoke on their jaws,
and I bent down to them and fed them.

They shall return to the land of Egypt,
and Assyria shall be their king,
because they have refused to return to me.
The sword shall rage against their cities,
consume the bars of their gates,
and devour them in their fortresses.
My people are bent on turning away from me;
so they are appointed to the yoke,
and none shall remove it.

How can I give you up, O Ephraim!
How can I hand you over, O Israel!
My heart recoils within me,
my compassion grows warm and tender.
I will not execute my fierce anger,
I will not again destroy Ephraim;
for I am God and not man,

the Holy One in your midst,
and I will not come to destroy.

They shall go after the Lord,
he will roar like a lion;
yea, he will roar,
and his sons shall come trembling from the west;
they shall come trembling like birds from Egypt,
and like doves from the land of Assyria;
and I will return them to their homes,
says the Lord.

Once again, it is the story of a God who loves first, and of a people which rejects God's love. Nevertheless, says the Lord, "I had good intentions. I looked for a combination of direction and love. I led you with cords of compassion and bands of love." One cannot assume another's suffering, but one can stay close to a sufferer. This is what God did by "easing the yoke on the jaws." Horses would appreciate this gesture. His people does not. Disappointment. Rage, the reverse side of love.

Then, Hosea describes a kind of conflict in God's conscience, "What should I do?" With His heart (reflecting in calmness) and His "stomach" (spontaneous feeling), God knows He should stay faithful to Himself, that is to say, to His love and His beloved. He is the Holy One in their midst, in spite of everything. To be holy means to be faithful. God will call His people back; the text speaks of Him "roaring." But this roaring is something like the remnants of rage which dissolve in love. It is akin to weeping for grief that is past. And they will come back home. God does not love because He is loved. He is the very first to love. Not once, but every time. He is always the first to love.

Powerless power. Powerless love.
Loving power. Powerful love.

God's Love Creates Liberty

Until now we have chosen our examples from the Old Testament. In part IV we shall study the New Testament, for it is in Jesus that God has most clearly demonstrated the (im)potency of love. Nevertheless, the data we have already collected suffice to illustrate that there is some such thing as the (im)potency of God's love in the face of human liberty, or, to put it another way, God is as weak and as strong as His love.

The Bible reveals that God is Love. Love presupposes freedom. If liberty is real, it includes the possibility of acting against love, a possibility which must be allowed to exist without any divine obstruction. This is the risk of freedom. To act against love, means to harm each other. In continuity with a long Christian tradition, Greshake writes, "If God wills created freedom into existence, then this necessarily implies the *possibility* of suffering."[46] He is joined by Schillebeeckx, "As soon as *creatures* exist, there is the *possibility* (not the *necessity*) of an originally negative 'initiative of finitude'."[47]

This affirmation puts God's omnipotence in a different light. Omnipotence does not mean that God's power overrules everything, even human freedom. God's omnipotence is the power of His love, which creates a space for human beings alongside God Himself, which endows men and women with freedom, and liberates them for its exercise. His power offers human beings opportunities for collaboration. It is a power which can be appropriated by human beings, and which can be "touched" by human freedom. Because God's omnipotence consists of His freedom and love, it does not oppress human persons or limit their capacities. The greatness of God's omnipotence is that it liberates human beings to freedom and to activity.

God's power is a liberating freedom (Galatians 5:1). A liberating freedom is powerful because it makes all the rest possible. As long as it remains faithful to itself, it does not impose anything. Such a liberating freedom offers everything, without obtrusiveness, since the receiver must accept in freedom, too. Häring expresses his conviction that in such an experience something is revealed of the liberating ground of all liberation, God Himself.[48]

---

[46] Greshake, "Suffering and the Question of God," 10.

[47] Schillebeeckx, "The Mystery of Injustice," 16.

[48] Hermann Häring, "Het kwaad als vraag naar Gods almacht en machteloosheid," *Tijdschrift voor Theologie* 26 (1986) 369-370.

Teilhard turns classic views upside down. Accord-
~ard should not be eliminated by trying to assume it
~s of nature. On the contrary, the laws of nature
~ towards freedom. If evolution realizes itself as a
~nt of freedom, then it does not occur according to
~ in play, in the testing of possibilities, in haphazard.
~et, creation — whose goal is the freedom of crea-
~not have the form of an orderly, well-appointed and
~peccable structure, but of dynamic, untrammelled,
~ovement. This, however, necessarily includes a
~he negative, disintegrating side of things, an abun-
~; in brief, all that leads to suffering. Teilhard actu-
~this context of "pain as a necessary by-product of
~eedom is already dearly bought in the sub-human
~evolution strides onward partly through experimen-
~rtly through strokes of luck, but, also, through labor
~Teilhard remarks:

~o its reflective zones we have seen the world proceeding
~of groping and chance. Under this heading alone — even
~uman level on which chance is most controlled — how
~res have there been for one success, how many days of
~ one hour's joy, how many sins for a solitary saint? To
~, we find physical lack-of-arrangement or derangement
~terial level; then suffering, which cuts into the sentient
~, on a still higher level, wickedness and the torture of
~analyses itself and makes choices. Statistically, at every
~evolution, we find evil always and everywhere, forming
~ing implacably in us and around us. *Necessarium est ut
~veniant*. This is relentlessly imposed by the play of large
~ the heart of a multitude undergoing organization ....
~nd failure, tears and blood: so many by-products (often
~moreover, and re-utilizable) begotten by the noosphere
~.... In one manner or the other it still remains true that,
~ view of the mere biologist, the human epic resembles
~much as a way of the Cross.[54]

~din, *The Phenomenon of Man*, 311-313.

This explains somewhat what we said above, when we remarked
that "omnipotence is a religious category." If one wishes to grasp
its real nature, one must think of it in terms of liberating relationship. God's power means that God goes on offering new opportunities, opening new paths to liberation, and relentlessly inviting us
to a creative evolution, so that ever more harmony is realized.

In 1846, Søren Kierkegaard (1813-1855) reflected on this kind
of omnipotence:

> The greatest good, after all, which can be done for a being, greater
> than anything else that one can do for it, is to make it free. In order
> to do just that, omnipotence is required. This seems strange, since it
> is precisely omnipotence that supposedly would make [a being]
> dependent. But if one will reflect on omnipotence, he will see that
> it also must contain the unique qualification of being able to with-
> draw itself again in a manifestation of omnipotence in such a way
> that precisely for this reason that which has been originated through
> omnipotence can be independent. This is why one human being
> cannot make another person wholly free .... There is a finite self-
> love in all finite power. Only omnipotence can withdraw itself at
> the same time it gives itself away, and this relationship is the very
> independence of the receiver. God's omnipotence is therefore his
> goodness. For goodness is to give oneself away completely, but in
> such a way that by omnipotently taking oneself back one makes the
> recipient independent. All finite power makes [a being] dependent;
> only omnipotence can make [a being] independent .... It is incom-
> prehensible that omnipotence is not only able to create the most
> impressive of all things — the whole visible world — but is able to
> create the most fragile of all things — a being independent of that
> very omnipotence. Omnipotence, which can handle the world so
> toughly and with such a heavy hand, can also make itself so light
> that what it has brought into existence receives independence.[49]

In the opinion of François Varillon, a fundamental choice needs
to be made between a God-Emperor and a God-of-Love. If one
chooses a God-of-Love, then "the game is open. There is a 'may
be'."[50] And if there is a *risque d'amour*, there is a *risque d'échec*.

[49] Howard V. Hong & Edna H. Hong (ed., transl.), *Søren Kierkegaard' Journals and Papers* (Bloomington and London: Indiana University Press, 1967-1978) vol. 2, no. 1251.
[50] François Varillon, *La Souffrance de Dieu* (Paris: Le Centurion, 1976) 28.

This is the dynamism of love. "To love means to promise and to promise each other never to use means of power vis-à-vis the beloved person. To reject the use of 'power' means to expose oneself to refusal, incomprehension, and unfaithfulness .... The only language which suits love is prayer. God does not 'will', He prays. To will implies power. To pray means to forsake power. To pray means to ask in fear and hope .... If a human being hears God's prayer, he reaches the summit of his existence."[51]

Liberty, Nature, and Finiteness

We have moved a step further in our reflections on the deeper meaning of ethical evil, that is to say, the sufferings that human beings bring upon each other. Precisely because God is Love, He confirms human liberty. If He revoked the gift of freedom, He would contradict his Love. Love does not use violence, and in this sense love is powerless. But, at the same time, love is powerful in its reliability and its capacity to set free. In this sense love and power are a little less contradictory.

There remains, however, another question, namely, the question of those miseries which do not flow from personal ethical sources, but from "nature" or from finiteness. This is sometimes referred to as physical and metaphysical evil. This question cannot be separated from the former one. There are many situations where ethical evil — because of its gigantic proportions — comes very close to (anonymous) evil from nature, situations where human beings are much more the victims than they are authors of evil. Ricoeur describes structural evil as hyper-ethical or transethical evil.[52]

We do not aim to pose yet again the question of the origin of evil from nature or from human finiteness. As we have already indicated, this question is insoluble. It starts from a false presup-

position, namely, that G
presupposition — to be
world! — amounts to a
obstructs all gratitude fo
possible.

The question we are
God's love, when confr
We will try to connect s
with human freedom. Fr
concern to link as close
and victims of evil, and
does not promote the st

From the perspective
Chardin (1881-1955) l
ideas. In his view, all th
This is Teilhard's interp
tion integrates the form
preliminary design of
development must be in
history of, the human le
design which is only f
human development (cc
dawning of that which r
freedom and conscience
becomes clear in the ph
mental law of creation i
freedom. In the hazardc
their various possibilitie
dictable complexity of p
inary steps of later hur
hazard is, in his opinion
of fuller realization.

In this way
ing to him, h
into strict la
should evolv
preliminary h
fixed laws, bi
From the out
tures — does
statistically i
and playful
shadow side,
dance of was
ally speaks i
evolution." F
sphere. Worl
tal tests and p
and loss — a

Right u
by mear
up to th
many fa
misery
begin w
on the r
flesh; th
spirit as
degree (
and refc
scandal
number
Sufferir
precious
on its w
even in
nothing

[51] Varillon, *La souffrance de Dieu*, 65-66. Varillon refers to Jean Lacroix, *Le désir et les désirs* (Paris: P.U.F., 1975) 79, 145.

[52] For this discussion, see Kristiaan Depoortere, "Mal et Libération: Une étude de l'oeuvre de Paul Ricoeur," *Studia Moralia* 14 (1976) 337-385, especially pp. 370-375.

[53] Pierre Teilhard de Chardin
Collins, 1965 - rev. edit.); D.
Understanding (New York: Pa

[54] Teilhard de C

Suffering: The Price of Love?

Teilhard's view is reminiscent of Kushner's: creation is unfinished. Nevertheless, we have moved a step forward: hazard is not mere chaos. Even unfinished business is not without its project. It can be understood as the preliminary design of a freedom which realizes itself in faithfulness and love. Greshake writes as follows:

> For our particular question about reconciling pain with the Christian concept of God, it emerges that the actual fact of suffering does not contain a complaint against the goodness of the Creator or the goodness of creation. Rather, our reflections lead us to see suffering as the price of freedom, the price of love. A God who used his omnipotent goodness to abolish all suffering would also abolish freedom, and with it love. As well as to postulate wooden iron, or a triangular circle, as love without suffering.[55]

Küng, Brantschen and many other authors strenuously oppose Teilhard and, in particular, his concept of "by-products." Greshake, although sympathetic to Teilhard's ideas, nevertheless quotes Dostoyevsky's *The Brothers Karamazov.* Ivan says to his brother Alyosha:

> I don't accept this world God has made. It's not that I reject God Himself, but this world of His I cannot and will not accept. Let me explain a bit better: like a child I am convinced that pain will heal and balance itself out ... But still I do not and will not accept this state of things! Too high a price is asked for harmony! My purse does not allow me to pay such an entry-charge. So I am in a hurry to give back my ticket.[56]

Brantschen proposes that we give up reasoning about "evil from nature," that we keep silent and assist the suffering, by helping them to bear their suffering. This is the only way to limit the damage caused by evil from nature. Indeed, the ethical evil provoked by humans (for example, the failure to assist the suffering) renders the suffering born of nature and structural suffering still more unbearable, and can alienate sufferers from their God. How can sufferers experience God's nearness without the closeness of fellow-humans?

[55] Greshake, "Suffering and the Question of God," 17.
[56] Quoted in Greshake, "Suffering and the Question of God," 18-19.

The Unmoved Mover: Suffering from Love?

How far have we come? We can at least entertain the possibility that suffering, even the suffering born of finiteness, need not constitute an accusation directed against God. God absolutely does not will suffering. Otherwise, He would not be God but a Moloch.

Why, then, does He not manifest His antipathy to suffering? He does, but not by a Moloch-act, that is to say, not by revoking the gift of freedom He bestowed upon His creatures and destroying those who oppose His love. God expresses His non-willing of suffering through an act of Love. This is the only way He can remain faithful to His divine nature. God is compassionate, committed to suffering people. He shares in the pain of the suffering people because He cannot stop loving. To enter into the suffering of humanity is the way He chooses to engage in the struggle against suffering. Very intense human experiences can suggest something of such a love. What do we do when we love someone who does not understand us? There is but one way: to love even more. Love can only be aroused by love. A human's heart can only be won by love, not by violence.

But what precisely does it mean to write that God shares in human pain because He is nothing but Love? This is a burning question in recent theology. Can we conceive of a suffering instead of a guiding or a ruling God? Can we conceive of a God who guides by compassion, through solidarity with the suffering? Is this an acceptable phrasing of the (im)potency of love?

Our classic image of God is shaped by the legacy of Aristotle (384-322). In Greek cosmology, the immutable substances are separated from the material ones and lifted above the world of becoming. There is no relationship between the Highest Substance (God) and the world that is in the process of becoming. The Unmoved Mover does not even know the world. To allow God to know the transient world would mean introducing variation and becoming into God.

It is quite obvious that such a radical immutability cannot be reconciled with Christianity, where incarnation occupies such a

central place. Therefore, all Christian theologians, especially
Thomas Aquinas (1225-1274), deal cautiously with the Aris-
totelian concept of The Unmoved Mover. This does not alter the
fact that it is hard for them to come to terms with concepts such as
becoming and change. In technical language, God is said to have a
relatio rationis (a relationship on the level of thinking), but not a
relatio realis, with the becoming world. To accept a real relationship would introduce time, finiteness, and contingency into God.
For Thomas, it is more perfect not to move than to move, and it is
more perfect not to have a relationship than it is to have one. It is
rather paradoxical: according to the Bible, God has created the
world; however, according to (some) theology, He should be situated radically outside and above time and space. According to the
Bible, He is a God of love and concern; without denying this
aspect, some theology, nevertheless, considers Him to be the
Unmoved. This image of God has exercised a great influence on
Christian culture.

It is, therefore, understandable that the first explicit descriptions
of God as a suffering God — that is to say, as a God who can be
'moved' — came as something of a theological shock. However,
since the appearance of Kazok Kitamori's *Theology of the Pain of
God*[57] in 1946, a number of theologians have pioneered this
approach. These include Jean Kamp,[58] Jürgen Moltmann,[59] Hans
Küng,[60] and François Varillon.[61]

---

[57] Kazok Kitamori, *Theology of the Pain of God* (London: SCM, 1966). Kitamori
applies a key-notion of Japanese tragedy to God. *Tsurasa* is the situation of someone who sacrifices him- or herself, or a beloved person, in order to save another.
It is essentially "the pain born of relationship."

[58] Jean Kamp, *Souffrance de Dieu et vie du monde*, L'actualité religieuse, no. 32
(Tournai: Casterman, 1971).

[59] Jürgen Moltmann, *The Crucified God: The Cross of Christ as the Foundation
and Criticism of Christian Theology* (London: SCM, 1974); *Trinität und Reich
Gottes: Zur Gotteslehre* (Munich: Kaiser, 1980); *Gott in der Schöpfung: Ökologische Schöpfungslehre* (Munich, Kaiser, 1985).

[60] Hans Küng, *Gott und das Leid* (Einsiedeln: Benziger, 1967); *Menschwerdung
Gottes* (Freiburg-Basel-Wien: Herder, 1970); "Die Religionen als Frage an die
Theologie des Kreuzes," *Evangelische Theologie* 33 (1973) 401-423.

[61] François Varillon, *La souffrance de Dieu* (Paris: Le Centurion, 1975).

Of course, this is a most complex question,[62] and one which needs to be situated in the framework of contemporary philosophical reflection. Contemporary philosophy no longer holds that it is more perfect not to have relationships than to have them. The positive sciences, too, support this thesis. They regard reality as relational; nothing exists in and for itself. A God who exists alone would be an abstract deity.

Starting from this thesis and step by step, many forgotten accents have been rediscovered. There is, for example, the following remark by Origen (3rd century): "Do you not know that God suffers? He suffers from love."[63] There are, too, texts from the Old Testament, such as those of Hosea. Varillon has undertaken a systematic investigation of those verses where God's weeping is mentioned. He concludes that, "This God in tears is the Holy One."[64] Varillon takes the motto which graces his book from Origen: "The Father Himself is not impassible." His study of the history of theology has brought to light a number of surprising expressions, which survived in the margins of an "unmoved" theology.[65] Greshake recalls that Jewish rabbinical theology affirms that God suffers where people suffer. And he concludes that if we take seriously the theme of God's love and concern, the idea of His incapacity to suffer can no longer be maintained.[66]

Jesus, the Suffering Son of God

The image of a com-passionate God, already hinted at in the Old Testament, is fully developed in the New Testament. In the person of Jesus, it is made clear that God truly enters into the suf-

---

[62] For a very complete treatment of the theme of the suffering God, see Paul Fiddes, *The Creative Suffering of God* (Oxford: Clarendon, 1988); Marc Steen, "The Theme of the 'Suffering' God: An Exploration," *God and Human Suffering*, ed. Jan Lambrecht & Raymond Collins, Louvain Theological and Pastoral Monographs, 3 (Leuven: Peeters, 1990) 69-93.

[63] Origen, *Homilies on Ezekiel*, 6,6.

[64] Varillon, *La souffrance de Dieu*, 32.

[65] Varillon, *La souffrance de Dieu*, 44-54.

[66] Gisbert Greshake, *Wenn Leid mein Leben lahmt: Leiden, Preis der Liebe?* (Freiburg im Breisgau: Herder, 1992).

fering world in order to combat pain. He meets the sick, he expels the powers of evil, and he suffers himself. In Luke 15:20, he is a suffering father, "He had compassion." The Greek word means that "the intestines are turned upside down and that the voice of the blood calls." The same verb is used in the scene of the dead boy at Nain (Luke 7:13). Jesus is "deeply moved in spirit and troubled" at the death of Lazarus (John 11:33,38) and weeps (11:35). There are many explicit identifications of Jesus with the poor and the suffering, summarized by Matthew 25:34-40:

> Then the King will say to those at his right hand, 'Come, O blessed of my Father, inherit the kingdom prepared for you from the foundation of the world; for I was hungry and you gave me food, I was thirsty and you gave me drink, I was a stranger and you welcomed me, I was naked and you clothed me, I was sick and you visited me, I was in prison and you came to me.' Then the righteous will answer Him, 'Lord, when did we see thee hungry and feed thee, or thirsty and give thee drink? And when did we see thee a stranger and welcome thee, or naked and clothe thee? And when did we see thee sick or in prison and visit thee?' And the King will answer them, 'Truly I say to you, as you did it to one of the least of these my brethren, you did it to me'.

Jesus, God's Son, himself enters into suffering: the road from the Mount of Olives to the Mount of Golgotha. He wishes to share even in the death of human beings. Death is the result of his mission, of his desire to share in the misery of the outcasts, of his transgression of social and religious taboos. Ultimately, it is the result of his claim, expressed precisely in his involvement and dedication, to be the only Son of God. The authorities wish to test this claim by means of an ordeal. If Jesus truly is the Son of God, then God should save him from the Cross. If God does not do this, then Jesus is a liar, and his claims are blasphemy. On Friday afternoon, Jesus appeared to be a blasphemer. "We knew it all along. Jesus is not the living Son of God. At least he is not the Son of the God we know."

Jesus is God's answer. Not the answer to the why-question. He is God's answer to the cry of suffering people. Through his voluntary com-passion, he sought to let suffering people know that they are never left alone. He sought to soften the senselessness of suffering by sharing in it. The Dutch poetess Vasalis wrote:

> So may kinds of sufferings,
> I don't call them by their name.
> Only one: to give up and to separate.
> And not the cutting hurts, but to be cut off.

Varillon reflects as follows:

> The concept of a passible God might be a scandal to reason, but the reality of an impassible God is revolting to the heart, which has its reasons too ....
> God is the eternal decision to love;
> thus to speak
> (if love, out of an essential desire, desires reciprocity, then love manifests itself and speaks; Jesus Christ is the Word);
> thus to pray
> (the Word is Prayer; in one unique movement God gives Himself and implores us to receive Him);
> thus — perhaps — to suffer
> (if love forsakes power which would impose its law, it exposes itself to rejection).[67]

If love possesses a specific power which we commonly call impotence, if perfection is no longer called power but love, if it belongs to God's perfection to be capable of suffering, then a very capital question remains unanswered. Is God still a leading God? Does God's com-passion — in the most literal sense of the word — have any effect? Certainly, a living experience of a close, dedicated, and compassionate God is important. But does His solidarity advance the struggle against suffering? In other words, is there a victory over suffering?

---

[67] Varillon, *La souffrance de Dieu*, 53, 75-76.

PART IV

THE POWERLESS SUPREMACY OF LOVE

In the first part of this study, we described the world of suffering people — so many kinds of suffering, suffering which people bring about and suffering which they undergo. From the beginning, we have insisted that we did not want to talk about suffering without struggling against suffering. To accompany people in their search for meaning is to engage in a kind of struggle against suffering. People inevitably seek meaning; human beings ask questions, and not just about suffering. They pose all-encompassing questions: Where do we come from? Why do we live? Where do we go? When he or she asks these questions, every human being — whether or not he or she is a believer — is confronted with the question of God's existence, either as a source of consolation or as a source of scandal.

In the second part of this book we tried to analyze the questions addressed to God, under the heading "Three Acquittals of God." We attempted to reflect on several concrete experiences of meaning with relation to suffering, and on the corresponding images of God. We distinguished three approaches: God as a fair Judge, God as a supreme Educator, and God as an inscrutable Being.

In the third part, "A God of Power and/or Love?," we moved from a more existential experience of meaning to a more theoretical attribution of significance. Leibniz' theodicy does not offer acceptable answers: God is so safely "protected" that both the living God and the concrete suffering person remain out of reach. Harold Kushner, on the contrary, asks many more direct questions at God. He — and other authors — refuse either to "protect" God any longer or to plead in His favor. If God is a true God, He should hear the cry of suffering people. Looking at Jesus, we think

He hears. At the end of the third part, we discovered the surprising image of a suffering God. However, another urgent question immediately arises: God may be compassionate, but what, then, of His power? Is there still a Power left to stop the powers of evil?

Our fourth part has two objectives. There is, first of all, a story. This is what may be described as an element of narrative theology. Christ incarnates the defenseless supremacy of Love that is God. Secondly, we ask what his story can mean today? How can the story of Jesus be revived in the care for suffering people? We move, then, from a more theoretical attribution of meaning to the concrete case of suffering people in their wrestling with God. As a prelude to these two reflections, however, we shall begin with a theological summary.

1. THE ITINERARY OF THE QUESTION OF SUFFERING

In a very clear article,[1] Adolphe Gesché sketches the different facets of the questions asked by suffering. He discerns five moments in the process of integrating suffering, which he designates with classical terms: *contra Deum, pro Deo, in Deo, ad Deum*, and *cum Deo*. Gesché's reflections can assist us in our attempt to develop a view of the powerless supremacy of God's love.

A Plea on Behalf of God

Unlike Gesché we consider the *pro Deo*-moment to be in the forefront. A plea on God's behalf is the most obvious approach to suffering on the part of the faithful. A person who believes tries to involve God in his or her real life. Faced with the negative aspects

[1] Adolphe Gesché, "Topiques de la question du mal," *Revue Théologique de Louvain* 17 (1986) 393-418. We have used the same article as the framework for our contribution in "You have striven with God: A Pastoral-Theological Reflection on the Image of God and Suffering," *God and Human Suffering*, ed. Jan Lambrecht & Raymond Collins, Louvain Theological and Pastoral Monographs, 3 (Leuven: Peeters, 1990) 211-234.

of life, a believer does not attack God directly. On the contrary — and this is typical of the *pro Deo*-moment — he or she defends, exonerates or acquits God. *Pro Deo*, in spite of suffering, the believer pleads on God's behalf. Earlier in this book we examined three versions of this approach: God as a fair Judge, God as the supreme Educator, and God as the inscrutable One.

The position adopted by (theoretical) theodicy is essentially *pro Deo*.[2] We have detailed the risks of such an approach. It can be seen as an attempt to assume the place of God. As far as suffering humans are concerned, there is the danger that these intellectualist and apologetic constructions will simply drown out their cries for deliverance. Hence, we are of the opinion that the *pro Deo* approach ultimately "blocks" the attribution of meaning. *Pro Deo*, but *contra hominem*.

A Complaint against God

An alternate response to suffering and to evil consists of a reaction against God, *contra Deum*. *Contra Deum* is the opposite of *pro Deo* but here, too, extremities very nearly meet. Both *pro* and *contra* relate suffering to God; each tendency moves in a different direction, however. In the "complaint against God" God is not defended or justified. He is accused or eliminated. *Contra Deum* is most clearly visible in its radical atheistic version: *malum, ergo non est Deus*: because of evil, God does not exist. If this atheistic vision were merely a rational argument, it could easily be invalidated by a demonstration of its internal logical contradictions.[3] In most cases, however, it concerns much more than cold logic. The *contra Deum* proposal is more a protest against a particular image of God, than against God as such. Moreover, it is as much a protest against suffering as it is against God. This is why this affir-

---

[2] Gesché, "Topiques de la question du mal," 398 refers to Vladimir Jankelevitch, *Le Pardon* (Paris: Aubier, 1967) 100-106: "La théodicée, philosophie du bilan (thème de l'harmonie de l'ensemble impliquant des déchets), accorde à Dieu les circonstances atténuantes!" (Theodicy - with its ideas about the harmony of the whole, despite waste products - attributes mitigating circumstances to God!)

[3] Gesché, "Topiques de la question du mal," 394-395.

mation should be taken seriously. Even believers must acknowledge its power. To believe would be much easier if there were no suffering. This kind of explicit or implicit atheism, unleashed by the reality of human suffering, not infrequently originates in lofty — and all too human — expectations of God. Disappointed expectations. Belief and unbelief can be born of disappointment. One could rightly ask if those who attack God — even to the point of denying His existence — perhaps do not have a more noble concept of Him than many of His defenders, who hardly feel up to a real confrontation with Him.[4] Such a *contra Deum* is not a closed question. It is born of a desire.

In God's Name

A closer look at the two preceding positions suggests that they are more preoccupied with God than with suffering people. These views talk "about" God, attacking or defending Him, eliminating or excusing Him. When the pleas have been entered, however, human beings are left alone with their suffering, and God has been left uncompromised by the problem of evil. He is either dismissed or lifted above the question. The God on whose behalf or against whom the plea is held, is not the living One. He is the god of the philosophers, a god "in itself" (*en soi*) or "for itself" (*pour soi*), but not the biblical "for us".

Instead of talking "about" God, Gesché suggests posing the question of suffering *in Deo*, and really relating it to Him. The author uses an image from the world of electronics: "Place the problem of suffering in God Himself and let suffering traverse God like a current traverses a resistor." The one who dares as much, soon discovers that God is already ahead of him or her. The problem of suffering is shown to be God's problem, because He did not spare his own Son (Romans 8:32). John the Baptist called Jesus the lamb of God who bears (*tollit*) the sins of the world. We should not hesitate to ask the question in a very radical manner.

---

[4] Ibid., 396.

"The last imprudence is the prudence which gently prepares us to do without God."[5] God is able to endure (*tollere*) the question. Not to ask direct questions also means to dismiss God. To pose the question *in Deo* means to take a human question so seriously that it becomes God's question.

An Appeal to God

If we really want to ask the question *in Deo*, we have to ask it *ad Deum*, to God, as Jesus did. *Ad Deum* starts when someone has "the courage to be afraid,"[6] when the person no longer closes his or her eyes to suffering, when he or she really allows it to enter into life. This is a fundamentally "pathic" moment. The sick person completely abandons any attempt at a dominant attitude. He or she calls for help. There are no limits to our inquiries: questioning (Why, Lord?), challenging (Where are you, God?), reproaching (If you were here, Lord), accepting (Thy will be done, Lord), imploring (Save me, God) and so forth. In a certain sense, *ad Deum* is the Christian *contra Deum*. *Ad Deum* neither swallows the question nor phrases it in the third person. *Ad Deum* changes the third person into a vocative, into direct address, and into a cry for help. A vocative is never a blasphemy.[7] This attitude moves from speaking "about" God and "about" suffering to speaking to God out of suffering. The fault of *contra Deum* is not the question itself, but its avoidance of the confrontation with the living God. Where God is addressed, human beings retain their dignity, their respect for God, and their legitimate questions. To speak is to believe in a presence. To believe in a presence is to believe in the possibility of an answer. To keep silent is to be closed in on oneself. To speak means to meet someone else. That someone might be wholly "other," one so different that He may even become an

---

[5] Georges Bernanos, *Journal d'un curé de campagne* (Paris: Plon, 1936) 115.

[6] See M. D. Molinié, *Le courage d'avoir peur* (Paris: Cerf, 1975).

[7] Gesché, "Topiques de la question du mal," 403 has an untranslatable play on words: "Sans maudire, non pas sans mot dire. En disant mot, en mot disant." (To remain silent is blasphemy because it is to stop talking to God).

Opponent[8], as Jacob discovered at the river side (Genesis 32:23-
33). Some psalms speak in this fashion. So did Jesus on the Cross:
"My God, my God, why hast Thou forsaken me?" (Mark 15:34)
This is a daring relationship, one which no longer attributes mitigating circumstances to God.

With God

At the end of a long journey, one may be surprised to discover
that God, too, asks the question of suffering, *cum Deo* —
together with God. As opposed to those theodicies which intro-
duced the idea of God's permissive will, the Bible reveals a
God who is scandalized by suffering. God's relationship to evil
is not a passive one (He neither permits evil nor is He incapable
of coping with it) but an active one. God is the adversary of
suffering. God's solidarity, first discovered as com-passion, turns
into more effective assistance: He acts together with human
beings against suffering. The Bible records God's struggle
against evil. If human beings fight suffering, they are not left
alone. God fights at their side (*cum Deo*). Why else should Jacob
have received a new name at the end of his fight with God,
"Israel, Fighter-by-the-grace-of-God"? (Genesis 32:29) Why, at
the end of the book, should God tell Job that his image of Him
was much more correct than that of his friends (Job 42:7)? The
answer would seem to be that the human struggle with suffering
is a divine affair. Evil is no longer an objection directed against
God (*contra Deum*); instead, God is an objection directed against
evil. This is what Job discovers: he had heard of God (in the
third person), but "now my eye sees thee" (42:5). Now Job
knows that God is on his side and that he is on God's side in a
common fight.

This is the meaning of prayer; it is a process of changing the
misery into a vocative, of praying for *con-fidence*: that the misery

[8] Ibid., 405: "Happy is the child who meets a person to strive with, all the better
if it is his or her father."

should be borne together (*cum*). God is His own theodicy, *Qui tol-lit peccata mundi*, not the One who "tolerates" or "permits" evil, but the One who "bears" it together with human beings, and will one day "carry it away". The most exact translation of John 1:29 reads as follows: "Behold, the Lamb of God who takes away the sin of the world." A lamb that triumphs over the powers of evil?

The discovery of the *cum Deo*-dimension of suffering does not mean the diminishment of one's humanity. On the contrary, it leads to the enhancement of that humanity. The person confronting evil is no longer alone. It is precisely evil's capacity to obscure the presence of both one's fellow humans and God Himself which constitutes its greatest power. This is the tragedy which is depicted in Franz Kafka's *The Trial*. In such a case, as Ricoeur writes, the human person is at once judge, accuser, and accused.[9] The First Letter of John affirms the very opposite: "By this we shall know that we are of the truth, and reassure our hearts before Him whenever our hearts condemn us; for God is greater than our hearts, and He knows everything"(3:19-20). Vergote quotes Dostoyevsky, "If God does not exist, everything is allowed."[10] Indeed it is, if God is seen as the Great Prohibitor. Vergote, however, goes on to quote the French psychoanalyst Jacques Lacan, "If God does not exist, then nothing is allowed." What Lacan means is that if there is no longer a God who supports us in our suffering and our freedom and helps us to bear them, human beings are doomed to the death of over-responsibility and guilt. In the words of Gesché, "*Il faut peut-être que vive Dieu pour que l'homme ne meure pas.*"[11]

With Christ

Gesché concludes his article with an observation which reignites the entire debate. One cannot talk about God without

---

[9] Ricoeur, *The Symbolism of Evil*, 144.

[10] Antoine Vergote, *Guilt and Desire: Religious Attitudes and Their Pathological Derivatives* (New Haven: Yale University Press, 1988) 46.

[11] Gesché, "Topiques de la question du mal," 415.

dealing with Jesus Christ. Too often, theology develops two distinct tractates, one on God the Creator and one on Christ the Savior. This inevitably leads to distortion. God is separated from Christ — His initiative of salvation. Moreover, classic theodicy barely asks questions *cum Christo*. In Leibniz's system, Christ is at most the eminent example of how evil might sometimes lead to a good which would not otherwise have found place.[12] Kushner's explicitly Jewish approach is, of course, developed independently of New Testament motifs.

If we insist on *cum Christo*, we do so quite intentionally. The affirmation which stands at the heart of Christian faith is that Jesus Christ is the Son of the living God. In Hebrew, Jesus means "God saves". Christ is the Greek word for Messiah, the Anointed. Jesus Christ is the Son of God, image and icon of the Father, his authorized representative, the visible figure of the Invisible One, the incarnated revelation of God's love for human beings. "To be the son of" is the strongest expression of a relationship. Christians use it to express the relationship between God the Father and Jesus Christ. The Creed describes Jesus the Christ as follows: "God from God, Light from Light, true God from true God." At the same time, it proclaims that "He became Man." Jesus is as close to humankind as he is to his Father. "The Word became flesh" (John 1:14). It cannot be expressed in a more literal way. Christ became a human being in time and space. He is fully God and fully Human.

Why are these affirmations so decisive? If Christ is not the Son of God, the rest of our story is no more important than the story of the life and death of any other martyr. But if Christ really is the Son of God, then God went through suffering and through death in his Son. If in Him "death has really died," then genuinely new horizons have been opened. One, at least, has reached the far shore, and God really is capable of a triumph over suffering and death. Then, our hope that God keeps His promises and calls all human beings across, is justified. Then, *cum Christo* really makes sense.

---

[12] Leibniz, *Essais de Théodicée*, I:10.

In what follows, we shall attempt to develop four themes. First of all, we shall reflect on the notion that Christ's passion is the story of God's closeness to suffering people. Through the ages, people have looked to the Cross of Jesus because they recognized themselves in his suffering. Secondly, we shall try to explain how Jesus' passion can be regarded as the story of triumph over sufferings. He went through death. Thirdly, we shall reflect on the promise contained in the story of Jesus, namely, that what happened to him is intended for all the faithful. All of us will be delivered from suffering. Fourthly, we shall consider the fact that this promise is inextricably linked to the task of fighting for life and against suffering and injustice. This is the full story: the "mystery of mercy" is much stronger than the "mystery of injustice." As Schillebeeckx expresses it:

> The 'mystery of injustice', which comes from the unfathomable depths of the tension between nature and our finite history of freedom, is seen to be weaker than the 'mystery of mercy' of the divine Event, which is the very essence of God, namely, the Father who is greater than all suffering because He conquers it. He is also greater than any theoretical or practical inability of creatures to finally experience the profoundest reality as an entrusted gift. We are in no position to provide a theoretical reconciliation of the two. The depths of what the negativity of finitude can (not 'must') mean, and the depths of what God's essential Positivity means, are always unfathomable."[13]

2. THE DEFENSELESS SUPREMACY OF LOVE

Jesus: The Story of God as a Fellow-Sufferer

Perhaps Luke's Gospel provides the best sketch of the popular movement Jesus provoked. The first nine chapters describe how ever more people are liberated from suffocating ties, and how they set out, having linked their lives and their lots to Jesus.

---

[13] Schillebeeckx, "The Mystery of Injustice," 18.

Every religion recognizes an almighty Creator of heaven and earth. Every believer bends his or her knee before Him in wondrous dependence. The Jews, however, once they had left the fleshpots of Egypt, became aware of a new interest, on the part of God, in the fortunes of human beings. He wanted to join them. He offered them an alliance. He allowed Himself to need people. He asked. The one who commands, makes other people vulnerable. The one who asks, becomes vulnerable. To ask means to expose oneself to the other's refusal. Many people answered 'no'. However, as the Old Testament makes clear, others consistently said 'yes'.

With Christ, the knowledge of God advances with a qualitative leap. The narratives of Jesus' birth and childhood are characterized by an uncritical simplicity. God chose to need a mother. He desired to become a child among human children. God asked this of Mary. She had many reasons to refuse. But she answered in the affirmative. In turn she became vulnerable. She became totally dependent on the love of others, of Joseph, for example. Her yes to God became a question to Joseph: "Will you also answer yes, even though you can hide behind the whole law and answer no?" Joseph answered yes, and he, in turn, became vulnerable, in the face of the innkeeper in Bethlehem, of Herod and of all those who say no.

Jesus is born. On the road. In a borrowed manger. With — according to the legend — an ox and a donkey. Two beasts of burden, beasts who do much work but know little appreciation. The Hebrew term is *sjorim chamorim*. Some languages have borrowed the word from the Hebrew. In Dutch, for example, the term *schorriemorrie* means riffraff. These are those who are too poor to be trustworthy, such as herdsmen. In Jewish tribunals they could not give evidence. Still, it is the riffraff who are called to be the first witnesses of Jesus' birth. Then there is the flight to Egypt, to an alien land, to someone else's land. They pass ancient pyramids; their flight, however, is the still more ancient lot of the poor and ·oppressed.

Nevertheless, the yes is contagious; the baptism in the Jordan, the call of the disciples; the crowd at the Mount; miracles of love and healing. Jesus warns: Your yes is not a romance. The seed falls into the soil and dies (Luke 8:4-15).

Luke 9 announces the turning turn of the tide. Jesus asks Peter, "Who do you say that I am?" Without any real awareness of what he is saying, Peter answers, "The Christ of God." Jesus commands him to tell this to no one because "the Son of Man will be rejected," and "all those who come after Him, will have to take up their cross" (Luke 9:18-27). Peter does not yet understand that love includes suffering. In 9:51, Luke's Gospel capsizes: "When the days drew near for Him to be received up, He set his face to go to Jerusalem." Jerusalem, the town of those who say no. Jesus chooses to meet his suffering. The Lukan word which is translated as "to be received up" (*assumptio; analèmpsis*) contains two dimensions: to be pulled up on the Cross and to rise to eternal life. Did Jesus already know it would be both?

In the next chapters, on the way to Jerusalem, we find brilliant pericopes about "putting one's hand to the plough and not looking back" (Luke 9:57-62), about children who discover real joy (10:21-24), about not knowing fear any more (12:4-12). There is the pericope of the ravens and the lilies (12:22-34), the story of the prodigal son (15:11-32), and the meeting with the rich young man who was left with nothing but his sadness, because he did not listen to the call of love (18:18-30).

Jesus draws near to Jerusalem. He reaches Jericho where Zacchaeus experiences that there is no more past, only future (19:1-10). Between Jericho and Jerusalem there is a desert. Across the desert lies the Mount of Olives. From its top one sees Jerusalem. At the foot of the Mount of Olives a crowd is gathered. Jesus is sitting on a borrowed colt. A poor man's entrance; only "ordinary" folk line the route (19:28-40). The constituted authorities wait near the temple, seeking asylum in his Father's house. A collision: "By what authority do you these things? What have you been saying about resurrection?" They all say no. All except one old woman at the back of the temple. The poor widow does what so many others did at the beginning: "She puts in all the living that she has" (21:1-4).

After the time of the yes, the time of the no begins. He whose life was solidarity is isolated. All his relationships are broken off. The passover is celebrated in a borrowed room. Only his disciples are left. He gives them the symbol of the Eucharist, "Do this in memory of me," do this in memory of my yes. A dispute arises among the disciples. John recalls how Jesus washes their feet (13:1-20), a variant of the Eucharist. Both symbols illustrate vulnerability; to be eaten and to perform slave labor. Even the intimate circle around Jesus breaks down. Not your enemies but your friends are able to hurt you. Judas leaves. Still, eleven remain.

They go to Gethsemane, the "olive press". Three of his disciples remain with Him. Jesus asks them to pray in solidarity. Jesus prays, "Not my will, but thine, be done" (Luke 22:42). The yes remains, a yes that is reminiscent of Mary's (Luke 1:38). Up until now his Father has been a Father. Will he call upon Him in vain? His disciples "were sleeping for sorrow."

Judas comes and betrays Him with a kiss, a symbol of love and solidarity. One of his disciples intervenes but, in a betrayal of the Sermon on the Mount, resorts to violence. Jesus is faithful to his preaching. There will be no violence. Even now he heals wounds. But Peter is swept away with those who say no. "Were you not with him?" No. Peter denies Jesus. Jesus does not deny Peter. "The Lord looked at Peter. Peter went out and wept bitterly" (22:61-62).

The elders of the people — the ones who know God — ask him about the only relationship left, "Are you the Son of God?" Jesus answers "yes". His ultimate relationship is called a blasphemy. For Pilate, however, blasphemy does not justify the death sentence. That is why the religious authorities attack the other sort of solidarity Jesus has displayed: "He perverts the people, saying that he is a king." "Yes," Jesus answers, "I am a king because I wash the feet of my fellow humans, because I practice solidarity with the lepers and the lame." Pilate becomes afraid of Jesus' unshakable yes. He looks for an escape route and sends Jesus to Herod, his archenemy. Strange detail, "Herod and Pilate became friends with each other that very day" (23:12). Jesus' healing work goes on. After the flagellation (another attempt at escape), Pilate allows the people to choose between Jesus and Barabbas (etymologically, the son of the father!). Pilate says yes and no in turn. It finally becomes a no. His career hinders his humanity. He washes his hands.

No reaches rock bottom. Sometimes, however, the lowly grow great in absolute misery. A strange procession. Jesus in the lead, Simon of Cyrene compelled to bear the cross-of-another. A timid yes is also a yes. And the crowd: the poor. They stay. Weeping women, impotence along the way of the cross of beloved persons. Do not underestimate the power of compassion. Jesus calls them "daughters of Jerusalem" (23:28), courageous women. Some people are called (or forced) to help, others to weep. Both are of equal importance. Two criminals, Jesus' company on the journey, bring up the rear. The long journey uphill.

On the mountain, Jesus prays. His Father is still there. By the power of his Father's presence Jesus forgives (23:34). But the process of isolation goes on. Soldiers cast lots to divide his garments. They mock him, "Save yourself." Another timid yes is spoken by one of the criminals, "Jesus, remember me" (23:41). "Truly, today we go home, for good." In an ocean of hate, forgiveness.

John mentions another yes under the Cross. Mary is there, his mother; John, his disciple; and Mary Magdalene. Three types of loves: parent-child, friendship, man-woman. His mother, a childless widow, will be condemned to marginality. Jesus says, "John, will you take her to your own home?" (John 19:25-27). A place of despair changes into a place of solidarity. Then darkness, clouds. The clouds of Moses at Sinai? The clouds of the inauguration of the temple of Solomon? The clouds of Jesus' baptism in the Jordan? The clouds of Mount Tabor? Symbols of God's creative work? Mark (15:34) and Matthew (27:46) report that Jesus cried, "My God, why hast thou forsaken me?" Complete isolation? The breaking off of his last relationship? Perhaps. Perhaps not. This is the first verse of psalm 22, a song which turns after the second half and becomes a song of trust and triumph, "You have saved me. I will tell it to all my brothers."

The curtain of the temple is torn in two (Luke 23:45), the curtain which separates the holiest places from "ordinary" people. It is torn in pieces. The entrance is free for widows, tax collectors, and lepers. God is accessible. "Father, into thy hands I commit my spirit" (23:46). His Father is still there. Jesus' last word is a vocative. At the end of his way of the cross, Job kept silent, astonished.

Jesus' yes is stronger than death. A new yes is spoken. A pagan centurion affirms, "Truly, this man was the son of God" (Mark 15:39; Matthew 27:54). One Roman corrects the faults of the other.

Another procession starts now; downhill. In the lead is Joseph of Arimathea, a member of the council. The council condemned him. Now, one of its members receives him. Soldiers undressed him. Now, he is clothed in a white garment. John reports Nicodemus' presence (19:39). The one who only dared to meet Jesus at night, is now publicly present. He runs the risk of impurity through contact with a dead body, immediately before the Sabbath. Jesus is dead. Nicodemus is born. Jesus is laid in a borrowed tomb. At sunset the Sabbath begins. The old law prevents embalmment. It will not be necessary. What revitalizing dialogue has found place between the suffering Son and his almighty Father, in the silent tomb during the Sabbath? The last Sabbath. "On the first day of the week, at early dawn, they went to the tomb ...."

Power: A Crucified Concept

This is the story of God as a fellow-sufferer. On Golgotha we can look at God's face, a bloodies and wounded head. Antique gods smile, beatifically. Socrates died aristocraticly. After having drunk the cup, he philosophized with his friends. Jesus died a brutal death. He asked not to have to drink the cup. He had no friends with whom he could engage in debate. Only a few relatives, broken by sorrow. After Golgotha, all-powerfulness is a crucified concept.

Elie Wiesel writes in *Night* [14]:

> The SS hung two Jewish men and a boy before the assembled
> inhabitants of the camp. The men died quickly but the death strug-
> gle of the boy lasted half an hour. 'Where is God? Where is He?'
> a man behind me asked. As the boy, after a long time, was still in
> agony on the rope, the man cried again, 'Where is God now?' And
> I heard a voice within me answer, 'Here He is — He is hanging
> here on this gallows.'

The God we meet here is not the classic, mighty ruler over the
world, responsible for everything and able to prevent any and all
suffering. The God we encounter is close to the sufferers. On the
Cross, Jesus' enemies cried, "If you save yourself we shall believe
that you are the Son of God." Our profession of faith asserts that
this Jesus who stays on the Cross is the Son of God, precisely
because he does not save himself and endures this injustice. He
identifies with the sufferers as the Compassionate One.

Paul Claudel expressed it as follows: "Jesus Christ did not
come to take suffering away from the world. He did not even
come to explain it. He came to fill suffering with his nearness."
Zahrnt writes, "Since Jesus' death on the Cross, I am absolutely
sure that God has never been on the side of the executioners. He is
always on the side of the sufferers." [15]

The cruelty of Jesus' death is not exceptional. Today, too, people die in intensive-care units, on battle-fields, and in slums. What
is exceptional is his confidence, although it had perhaps been
shocked more than any other person's.

> Jesus experienced what it means to be rejected by everyone, and
> this experience reached into the depths of his soul. Perhaps he did
> not suffer more physical pain than other human beings. However,
> because of his exceptional solidarity with humankind and with
> God, because he called God his Father in a way no human had
> ever done, because he sacrificed his life for his fellow humans like
> no human ever did, because of these things he must have felt what
> it means to be abandoned by God and by everyone. In this aban-
> donment, however, he calls upon God and throws himself in his

[14] Elie Wiesel, *Night* (New York: Hill and Wang, 1960) 70.

[15] Zahrnt, *Wie kann Gott das zulassen?*, 74.

arms. This means that Jesus' experience of God's Fatherhood persisted, even in suffering. Or, to be more precise, his experience of God as a Father carried him through suffering. Throughout all the shocks that marked the end of his life, one thing remained stable: God's faithfulness and Jesus' confidence.[16]

Nevertheless, nobody would ever have spoken of his death, if there were not these events which the faithful call resurrection.

Jesus: Passage through Suffering and Death

Not to feel alone; to realize that my suffering, however intense, is exceeded by the suffering of others; this can be a kind of consolation. To believe that the Son of God suffered and died can also be a source of consolation. But, what is the rest of the story?

The rest of the story tells of God's victory over suffering, His passage through suffering; it tells of the salvation that followed upon suffering. Schillebeeckx writes as follows:

> The 'initiative' of finitude [that is to say, the contradiction of love and the source of suffering], is an initiative that absolutely, originally, and exclusively derives from the finite, without any assistance from God. Such a negative initiative which indirectly plays a role within the positive human life which God supports, nevertheless, does not checkmate God. However, it is my opinion that we can in no way know this on the basis of a general notion of God, but only through the 'God of Jesus', namely, from a Christian belief in the resurrection. Thus it is apparent that God transcends these negative aspects in our history, not so much by allowing them, but by conquering them and un-doing them. The resurrection is, in essence, a correction, a conquering of the negativity of suffering and even death.[17]

At least twenty years after the events, Paul writes as follows to the community at Corinth:

> I delivered to you as of first importance what I also received, that Christ died for our sins in accordance with the scriptures, that he was buried, that he was raised on the third day in accordance with the scriptures, and that he appeared to Cephas, then to the twelve. Then he appeared to more than five hundred brethren at one time,

[16] Ibid., 71-72.
[17] Schillebeeckx, "The Mystery of Injustice," 17.

> most of whom are still alive, though some have fallen asleep. Then
> he appeared to James, then to all the apostles. Last of all, as to one
> untimely born, he appeared also to me. (1 Corinthians 15:3-8)

Nevertheless, on Friday afternoon the authorities seemed to have been proved right. The ordeal on the Cross did not issue in Jesus' vindication. God did not save his "son." On Saturday, when Jesus was locked up in the tomb, the disciples were locked in the upper room, the room of the remembrance of lost alliances.

Paul provides a very factual report of the events of Sunday morning. For those concerned, however, it must have been a strenuous struggle with doubts. A slow climb out of despair. Did they climb or were they pulled? Jesus "imposed" himself upon the disappointed disciples. Against all evidence. The disciples were resigned to the facts; Jesus was dead. The four Gospels tell of women who went to the to tomb in order to embalm the corpse. It is certain that nobody expected a resurrection. Jesus disturbs their evolution towards acceptance and resignation. He breaks through the closed doors of despair. Only later do they remember that, "He had told them long before ...."

Very nearly the entire Gospel of Luke is an uphill movement, a climb towards Jerusalem. On the third day, a reverse movement starts, away from Jerusalem. The community around Jesus bursts apart. Two disciples go back home to Emmaus (Luke 24:13-35). John suggests that the other disciples resume their former jobs in the north, near the Lake. They all seem to be on the road of the past, away from a beautiful dream. But there is an incident. The women discover the tomb empty.

> When the Sabbath was past, Mary Magdalene, and Mary the
> mother of James, and Salome, bought spices, so that they might go
> and anoint him. And very early on the first day of the week they
> went to the tomb when the sun had risen. And they were saying to
> one another, 'Who will roll away the stone for us from the door of
> the tomb?' And looking up, they saw that the stone was rolled
> back; for it was very large. And entering the tomb, they saw a
> young man sitting on the right side, dressed in a white robe; and
> they were amazed. And he said to them, 'Do not be amazed; you
> seek Jesus of Nazareth, who was crucified. He has risen, he is not

here; see the place where they laid him. But go, tell his disciples
and Peter that he is going before you to Galilee; there you will see
him, as he told you.' And they went out and fled from the tomb;
for trembling and astonishment had come upon them; and they
said nothing to any one, for they were afraid. (Mark 16:1-8)

In the midst of these centrifugal forces, there appears a quiet
person, a stranger. John (20:11-15) reports that Mary stood weeping outside the tomb, "They have taken the Lord away." She
turned around and saw the gardener, "Tell me where you have laid
my deceased Lord." In John 21:4, a stranger, near the Sea of
Tiberias, asks for some fish. He is hungry. But they had not caught
any fish. There is nothing left; their Lord is dead. In Luke, the dis-
ciples-on-the-way-back to Emmaus meet a stranger too, "Can I
walk with you?" Three times a stranger. Three times a lost person.
Nobody recognizes him. They are looking for a dead person and
do not see the Living One. Their community falls to pieces. They
don't see that Jesus is alive, that he keeps them company, even on
the way back.

Then the tide turns again. In John 20, the gardener takes the initiative. "Mary," he says. In the midst of despair, she is called by
her name. "Rabboni," she answers. Mary Magdalene is the very
first person to recognize Jesus — although, in Jewish jurisprudence, the testimony of women was as feeble as that of herdsmen.
"Do not hold me," Jesus says to her. Is he really the same as
before? "Do not hold me, for I have not yet ascended to the
Father; but go to my brethren and say to them, I am ascending to
my Father and your Father, to my God and to your God" (20:16-
17). He is the same Lord, but different. He is not the One who
returned from death. He is risen. He is fully grown and perfect.
His relationship with humans will be different, more intense. He
will no longer be "with" them or "next" to them. He will live
"in" them. As long as he was physically present, he was sometimes absent. Now he will always be present *intimior intimo*. He
himself reveals the secret: the discovery that "My father is your
Father." Mary has to discover a much more profound relationship
than the one she has enjoyed up to now. If she allows Jesus to live

in her, she will be capable of saving and healing relationships. "Go to my brethren" and tell them that it was not in vain that I went on calling God my Father.

The same turn is evident in the Emmaus story. On the long journey back, "their eyes were kept from recognizing Him" (Luke 24:16). Of course, it is night when they arrive. In spite of their sadness, they ask the stranger to stay with them. Without being fully conscious of what they are doing, they say a little yes to a lost person. Without being fully conscious of what they are doing, they execute Jesus' last will and testament; they share everything they have, even on the way back. Not the host but the guest breaks the bread. "Their eyes were opened and they recognized him." The story immediately continues, "they recognized him and he vanished out of their sight" (24:31). Reasons enough to be depressed. Instead, however, "they rose that same hour and returned to Jerusalem." In a lost stranger they recognize the Lost One. When the Lost One becomes a friend, he vanishes from their sight. They have to rise and to go out in order to recognize the Friend in other lost persons. Just like Magdalene, the disciples of Emmaus have discovered the play of the Present-Absent.

In a collection of verse which bears the title, *Adagio*, the Flemish poet, Felix Timmermans, writes as follows:

> Lord, stay **with** us, the day is so far spent.
> We shared our evening bread
> with the stranger,
> who had journeyed with us along the road.
> And while he blessed it, his eyes closed,
> it happened: His face was illumined
> by a heavenly light,
> in which he suddenly disappeared...
> This was a wonder.
> We were alone again,
> but with joy we joined our hands.
> It was as if He had vanished through us
> and the light in us continued to shine.
> Lord, stay **in** us, the day is so far spent!

The disintegration of communities; an encounter with the risen Lord; the building up of new communities. These are the three moments of faith in resurrection.

Let us return to John 21, to a place near the lake-of-the-past. The stranger on the bank calls, "Try again, cast the net on the right side." They catch a hundred and fifty-three fishes (21:11). "A hundred and fifty-three" means every possible kind of fish, every possible people on earth. A universal community to be built up. But the disciples do not yet know this. A surprising detail: "When they got out on land, they saw a charcoal fire there, with fish lying on it and bread" (21:9). Again, the same turn of events as in Emmaus: the guest becomes the host, the poor man distributes food, the hungry one serves the meal, the one who is lost brings others together.

The Gospel according to John finishes with a threefold question to Peter. The threefold 'no' spoken during Jesus' passion becomes a threefold declaration of love, a threefold yes. "Go now, Peter and gather together a hundred and fifty-three isolated people around the Lord."

Easter: The Answer to Good Friday

Passover — exodus and passage through — is God's answer to Good Friday. Easter does not explain suffering in order to make it a little more bearable. Easter triumphs over suffering. Easter changes suffering into life. Küng writes, "Where the story of Job ends, the Gospel of Jesus Christ begins. To Job was revealed the incomprehensibility of a merciful God. A human person should believe even if he or she does not understand. Through the Cross of Jesus Christ the mercy of the incomprehensible God has been revealed."[18]

For Schillebeeckx, the resurrection of Jesus means at least three things.[19] In the first place, resurrection means a divine ratification of Jesus' Abba-experience. Even face to face with death, Jesus

---

[18] Küng, *Gott und das Leid*, 52.
[19] Schillebeeckx, "The Mystery of Injustice," 17.

addresses God as his Father. This vocative deprives suffering and death of their power to separate him from his Father. For this is what death as such certainly is: the victory of the powers of separation and isolation. In suffering and death human beings run the risk of losing, at the same time, their lives and their God. Jesus' resurrection confirms that it was not in vain that he went on calling his God "Abba-Father." Even death was not capable of separating him from his Abba.

Secondly, resurrection is the divine ratification of Jesus' devotion to his fellow humans. Jesus' resurrection is a divine approval of his unselfish love and his perilous struggle against suffering. Jesus went on loving, to the death. Resurrection is the confirmation that such a love is not lost. In a human's devotion to his or her fellow humans, failure will no longer have the last word. Jesus dies but he did not Die. The scene with Thomas (John 20:24-29) illustrates this: Jesus appears with the scars of his wounds. He is the same Lord, but the wounds no longer bleed.

In the third place, resurrection symbolizes a divine correction of the negativity of suffering and death. Jesus' resurrection is a correctional "elevation," a new creation, a new covenant, in which all negativity is overcome in a life after death. In the resurrection, life acquires its ultimate identity. Resurrection proves that God cannot be thwarted by the misuse of human liberty. Easter is the passage from human (im-)possibilities to God's possibilities. In Christ the supremacy of God's love is confirmed.

Jesus: The First-Born

We know the outcome of Jesus' history of life and love. Does this outcome have any effect on our history of suffering? It does, if it is true that Jesus of Nazareth is the Christ, the Son of God, inextricably Human and God. It all depends on this. If he is only God, there is no guarantee that what happened to him will happen to us, too. But if he really is God and Human Person, then new horizons, new perspectives, are opened. The Scriptures do not hesitate. Jesus is called the Son of God, the First-Born of humankind, or the Head of the Body. The head has already been born. The body will follow. In the meantime, human beings live and suffer while they draw life from this promise: what happened to Jesus will happen to them, if they go on calling God "Abba." This is Saint Paul's testimony:

> We are afflicted in every way, but not crushed; perplexed, but not driven to despair; persecuted, but not forsaken; struck down, but not destroyed; always carrying in the body the death of Jesus, so that the life of Jesus may also be manifested in our bodies. For while we live we are always being given up to death for Jesus' sake, so that the life of Jesus may be manifested in our mortal flesh .... Knowing that He who raised the Lord Jesus will raise us also with Jesus and bring us with you into his presence. (2 Corinthians 4:8-11,14)

So, too, in the letter to the Philippians (3:10-11):

> That I may know him and the power of his resurrection, and may share his sufferings, becoming like him in his death, that if possible I may attain the resurrection from the dead.

Resurrection is and remains a promise, not a right we can claim. Resurrection is not born of human power, but of God's all-powerful love. Belief in the resurrection includes a long and painful process of mourning, and the abandonment of many all-too-human fantasies about immortality. Being able to believe in the resurrection presupposes the courageous acceptance of our finiteness and mortality. It is only then that a God can appear who makes everything new, the Other in His incomprehensible otherness, the absolutely free God who offers us — simply out of love — the unimaginable gift of a re-creation. Human beings bear an endless longing which, because of their mortality, they cannot satisfy. That God will transform our mortality into immortality and assume our infinite longing in His infinitude, is His gift — a miracle of His love and freedom, and not our right.

Paul describes the sufferings he endured for the Gospel: "But I do not deserve anything. All I have done was given". "If I must boast, I will boast of the things that show my weakness .... The Lord said to me, 'My grace is sufficient for you, for my power is made perfect in weakness.' I will all the more gladly boast of my weakness, that the power of Christ may rest upon me" (2 Corinthians 11:30; 12:9).

It is not that easy to believe because resurrection turns everything upside down. How can the Crucified One save? How can love be over-powerful? Paul continues: "Jews demand signs and Greeks seek wisdom, but we preach Christ crucified, a stumbling block to Jews and folly to Gentiles, but to those who are called, both Jews and Greeks, Christ the power of God and the wisdom of God. For the foolishness of God is wiser than men, and the weakness of God is stronger than men" (1 Corinthians 1:22-25).

Merciful, not Merciless

What God has said in the resurrection of Christ, He says to all the faithful.

In the first place, the promised resurrection will ratify their Abba-experience. If human beings continue to call God "Father," in spite of all appearances to the contrary, then the divisive powers of suffering and death will not be able to separate the children from the Father. This is at least Paul's conviction:

> If God is for us, who is against us? Who shall separate us from the love of Christ? Shall tribulation, or distress, or persecution, or famine, or nakedness, or peril, or sword? No, in all these things we are more than conquerors through him who loved us. For I am sure that neither death, nor life, nor angels, nor principalities, nor things present, nor things to come, nor powers, nor height, nor depth, nor anything else in all creation, will be able to separate us from the love of God in Christ Jesus our Lord. (Romans 8:31,35,37-39)

In the second place, the promise of resurrection confirms a human person's devotion to his or her fellows. Nothing of what human beings do to each other, will perish, as Matthew 25 asserts.

In the third place, resurrection constitutes the final and decisive correction of suffering and death. The Revelation to John guarantees this image of the future:

> Then I saw a new heaven and a new earth; for the first heaven and
> the first earth had passed away, and the sea was no more. And I
> heard a great voice from the throne saying, 'Behold, the dwelling
> of God is with men. He will dwell with them, and they shall be his
> people, and God Himself will be with them; He will wipe away
> every tear from their eyes, and death shall be no more, neither
> shall there be mourning nor crying nor pain any more, for the for-
> mer things have passed away.' (21:1,3-4)

The ultimate horizon of human existence will not be mercilessness
but mercy.[20]

3. A SPIRITUALITY OF CONFIDENCE AND RESISTANCE

A last and very important question remains: how can we come
to a concrete experience of meaning in our personal lives, and how
can we help others persons to discover it?

From "Why" to "With Whom?"

According to Greshake, Christian hope in the final victory over
suffering and death, begins here-and-now, in the performance of
little signs of hope. "Christian hope does not focus only upon the
End (as terminal point) but on the Fulfillment which is already at
work, and which manifests itself through anticipatory 'minor' ful-
fillments."[21] These anticipatory signs must be made real in our
own personal lives and in the lives of our fellows.

In this meantime, the question of suffering will neither be "Why
so much suffering?" nor "Where does suffering come from?"
(understood as a retrospective search for an "evil principle" or a
pre-given "order" of which human beings are victims). Kushner
rightly puts the question to be asked, as follows: things being what
they are, what can we do about them? This is an active and
prospective question: what can we do about suffering? The his-

---

[20] Zahrnt, *Wie kann Gott das zulassen?*, 68.
[21] Greshake, "Suffering and the Question of God," 22-23.

tory of Jesus offers us an unambiguous answer. The outcome of his life is promised to all the faithful. This is the question of the final Hope, of the Future (*l'avenir*). By posing this question, however, we also ask the question of our more limited hopes (*le futur*) — what can we do now? "What shall we do now that this has befallen us?" "Whom can we help and how?" "To whom can I give a cup of cold water?" "How can I change structures which provoke oppression?" The final conquest of suffering by Christ does not relieve us of the struggle against suffering. Were this the case, faith really would be opium.

Schillebeeckx reflects on the way in which the christological moment of the resurrection includes an ecclesiological dimension:

> That Jesus is risen, means not only that he is awaken from death by the Father, but, at the same time, (and just as essentially), that God gives him, in the dimension of our history, a community or church, and to the Apostles He gives an Easter-experience .... Through his resurrection, Jesus is personally present with his disciples in an entirely new manner .... The Easter-experience consists of the re-assembly of the disciples, not only 'in the name' of Jesus, but also clearly experienced as an event deriving from 'the power of' the risen Jesus himself. Where two or three are gathered in his name, Jesus is in the midst of them. Probably this is the most pregnant expression of the Easter-experience. The resurrection of Jesus and the re-assembly of the disciples (or 'becoming a church') are, on the basis of the resurrection faith, two real aspects of the single great salvific action.[22]

Schillebeeckx continues as follows:

> Resurrection is, at the same time, the sending of the Spirit, and thereby the founding of the church, that is, renewed fellowship of life of the personally living Jesus with his own on earth. In this way, the personal resurrection of Jesus, and ecclesial mysticism, and engagement on earth in the conquest of the human history of suffering are all internally connected.[23]

The experience of the risen Christ immediately turns into a new mission. The risen Christ is not an object of noncommittal con-

---

[22] Schillebeeckx, "The Mystery of Injustice," 23-24.
[23] Ibid., 25-26.

templation. On the basis of her belief in Christ's resurrection, a faithful community is obliged to take care of the poor and the suffering. Caring for the poor and the suffering, the biblical widows and orphans, involves four dimensions: (1) the necessity of a personal view of life; (2) the formation of a community with the sufferers; (3) the relationship with God; and (4) the function of prayer and liturgy.

A Personal View of Life

Suffering always challenges workers in health care to reflect on their personal view of suffering and, more globally, of life.

Jesus' comments on the incident of the human blood mingled with sacrifices by Pilate are very penetrating: "Do not ask why this happened to the victims. Ask questions of yourself. Ask yourself where you endanger the life of other persons. Repent" (Luke 13:1-5). His comments are immediately followed by the parable of the infertile fig tree. Every instance of being shocked by suffering in the world should be accompanied by a reflection on our personal commitment. It ought to include a realistic awareness of where we cause suffering.

A realistic questioning of our personal commitment requires of us that we strive to link our roles as both authors and victims of evil. In general, human beings are both. Zahrnt sketches this process of growing awareness in three stages. Initially, one experiences suffering as a fatality. On the next level, there is a growing recognition of one's personal contribution to this fate, guilt. Only the third step, however, is fully realistic: the suffering world is a mingling of fate and guilt. Personal guilt is experienced as a fate to which human beings actively contribute.[24]

It is a matter of recognizing one's personal role in guilt as honestly as possible, and of taking it upon oneself. The Flemish author, Frans Cromphout, expresses it as follows in *Kyrie*[25]:

---

[24] Zahrnt, *Wie kann Gott das zulassen?*, 81-82.
[25] Albert Boone, Frans Cromphout, *Kyrie* (Tielt: Lannoo, 1971) 29.

My sin testifies against me
that I am not human.
This is why I prefer to forget my guilt,
which makes me empty and sad,
small before You,
and before myself.
I prefer to stand upright,
testifying against my guilt,
that it is a shadow,
we have invented out of fear.
But I lose myself,
if I deny my guilt,
past and future disappear.
I am lost without my guilt.
It made me:
burnt place in the forest
razed houses,
ruins, hole, void,
where You can stream in.
My sin, God, testifies
I am human.

A person who is not capable of recognizing his or her own part in suffering cannot help other people to admit their guilt. The one who systematically avoids the suffering connected with this kind of admission of guilt will not be able to support his or her fellow humans. Moreover, his or her will to be concerned about another's suffering will inevitably be paralysed. Contemporary society, with its unreal fantasies about welfare, happiness, relationships, and so forth, does not encourage the sharing of sufferings. On the contrary, it discriminates against those who do not reach its illusory "ideal."[26] However, only those persons who have come to terms with their own limits and have experienced moral, physical, and metaphysical evil without yielding, will be able to help other humans when they are confronted with their limits. Those who have cleverly avoided the struggle, those who have never striven with God, as Jacob did, will never be capable of drawing near when people cry, "My God, why hast Thou forsaken me?" They do not know psalm 22, neither its first nor its last verses.

[26] Zahrnt, *Wie kann Gott das zulassen?*, 82-84.

Solidarity in the Struggle against Suffering

Suffering not only challenges our personal view of life; it also calls us to solidarity in the struggle against suffering. For the believer, this is a matter of the credibility of faith. God's care for the sufferers is "realized" in the support people give to each other. To assist each other means at least three things: protest, solidarity, and consolation.

To protest is to lend one's voice to those who do not have the capacity to cry out. Where protest transcends the level of selfish claims, and seeks to break through the crust of habit and narrow-mindedness in order to expose the whole truth, it loses its negative character. To protest in the name of another is to perform a prophetic function. In a hospital, for example, such a prophetic deed can be called for when curing supplants caring, when a prolongation of life turns into a prolongation of suffering, when ethical decisions are reduced to their medico-technical aspects, when reorganization only hits the patients or the low-skilled personnel, when the poor are victims of discrimination, when no information is given to patients or to their relatives, when there are no facilities for families, when professional confidentiality is violated, when the weakest life is only valued according to standards of productivity, when suffering and death have become routine, and so forth.

Protest is a kind of solidarity; but one voice, alone, is feeble and vulnerable. The united voices of a group cannot be overlooked that easily. Between guilty silence and outright revolt, there is much room for prophetic maneuver.

Arthur Koestler (1905-1983)[27] developed an interesting perspective on ethical engagement and its risks, particularly when the fighter is left alone. According to Koestler, history evolves by means of an interaction between four symbolic factors. On the one side are the Proletarian and the Prophet. On the other side are the Yogi and the Police Commissar.

---

[27] Arthur Koestler, *Darkness at Noon* (Harmondsworth: Penguin, 1946); *Le Yogi et le Commissaire* (Paris: Charlot, 1946).

The Proletarian, the symbol of the silent, oppressed crowd, constitutes an enormous potential power. If the Proletarian — literally, the one to whom nothing is left but his or her progeny (*proles*) — genuinely responds to a situation of continuous exploitation, the world will topple. The Proletarian exerts a constant pressure on the conscience of humankind. He or she is the world's *scruple* (literally, a little stone in a shoe). Emmanuel Levinas would probably call him or her "the naked face of humankind." The Proletarian and the Prophet are brothers. If the Proletarian is the horizontal power of history, the Prophet is its vertical dimension. The Prophet is the eye of the crowd in movement. Prophets call down justice from heaven. They are the living reminders of values. This is why they inspire and fructify the Proletarian. Prophets channel the energy of a people in a certain direction. However, they do this without resorting to power. They work slowly, and patiently, but irresistibly. The Proletarian needs the vision of the Prophet in order to choose the direction in which he or she should move. The Prophet needs the feet of the Proletarian in order to march. The people and its prophets are a unity of movement and goal, power and direction.

All too often, however, the Prophet loses contact with the Proletarian. The Prophet is too far ahead or too far behind. The Proletarian no longer understands the Prophet. The Prophet without the Proletarian loses touch with reality; he or she becomes isolated, and withdraws despairingly into a closed world. The Prophet becomes a Yogi. While the Yogi's intentions may be quite pure, however, his or her navel is the center of the world. It is at this point that the Proletarian loses his or her vertical dimension and inspiration. The Proletarian, too, becomes hopeless. If the Prophet turns into a Yogi, the Proletarian changes into a Police Commissar, the (Marxist) symbol of bold violence. The Commissar writes history with the blood of other people.

Commissars are Proletarians in despair. They use violence in order to achieve at least something; but, in their choice of means, they betray the goal.

The third dimension of solidarity can be called consolation. Protest and prophetic solidarity reveal their authenticity in their capacity for consolation. In the midst of large-scale ideals, the helpless neighbor is not overlooked. The practitioners of such solidarity are ever ready to offer a cup of cold water, even where this 'diversion' seems to constitute an ineffective loss of time and energy or a distraction from the grand design. The task of the weeping women on the road to Golgotha is indispensable. They symbolize the concrete powerless-powerful closeness to one single sufferer. The task of consolation is often not reducible to a specific function. It is, instead, a quality which changes a technical act into a human one by investing it with a new dimension.

Christian assistance will always be paradoxical, both on the macro or organizational level, and on the micro level of concrete deeds. It is an attempt to invest (financial and organizational) rationality with the irrationality of love and compassion.

A Living Relationship with God

To assist the suffering, we need not only a global personal view of life (one which addresses the questions of meaning), but a deepening of our personal relationship with God. One of the aims of our journey in faith with the sick and the suffering is the promotion of a living relationship with God. One cannot offer what one does not first possess.

Faith, however, is not a spontaneous process. To learn to pronounce a faithful yes to our imperfect reality — particularly when we are confronted with suffering — is by no means easy. This faithful yes is sober. It is a yes-in-spite-of, a yes-through-the-pain, a yes-that-pain-might-cease. Such a faith presupposes a process of renunciation, the setting aside of many powerful phantasms (concerning God, life, fellow humans, and especially concerning ourselves), a stubborn attention to the things which are nevertheless possible, a step by step discovery of the fact that a human being, in spite of everything, seems to be borne through life, and a gradual hearing of an invitation to commend oneself to a Mystery which unfolds according as one abandons oneself to it.

In this manner, a believer's yes becomes a vocative, an appeal addressed to Someone who is more original than my origins, more ultimate than my goals. Still, in the shadow of suffering this yes remains a prayer of petition. It is appropriate that the last verses of the New Testament (even after everything has happened, even after the fulfillment brought by Christ!) express a demand, "Maranatha: Come, Lord Jesus!" and a wish, "The grace of the Lord Jesus be with all the saints. Amen." (Revelation 22:20-21)

According to Zahrnt, a faithful yes will always be an "oh, yes" because the question of suffering is not an exam question. It is just the opposite. The person who does not answer the question is right. This, however, does not mean that vital questions should be brushed aside. On the contrary, not to answer them means to continue asking them. As soon as one stops asking them, either by giving an answer à la Leibniz or by regarding them as definitely unanswerable, one fails.[28] Precisely because the question of suffering cannot be answered and should not be left unanswered, the believer is moved to turn to the hidden God and invited to repeat, again and again, "and yet, Lord." This is an Amen born, at once, out of both confidence and resistance.

"To be confident, in spite of everything" is the most authentic meaning of the notion of God's providence. In the Bible, this expression is found in Genesis 22:14, where Abraham calls the place of Isaac's sacrifice "The Lord will provide" (*Moriah*). In this sense the term "providence" expresses a courageous confidence, a confidence which constitutes the foundation of human commitment.

The word "providence", when used in relation to human liberty, is particularly charged. This is especially true when it is employed in a chronological sense, as if "God already knew in advance." In its more authentic meaning, the word is simply a variant of the Name of Yahweh, the caring, concerned God. This,

---

[28] Zahrnt, *Wie kann Gott das zulassen?*, 84.

however, does not contradict the fact that the expression "divine providence" *quoad nos*, when applied to us, might sometimes include a retrospective dimension. On occasion, subsequent to a significant event in our lives, we can truly say, "This was so decisive that I cannot but conclude that God was at work here." However, this conclusion tells us more about human post-vidence than about divine pro-vidence. If this reading of our personal history promotes still greater trust, it is meaningful. This kind of reinterpretation can be compared to Moses' experience at Sinai. Just before the conquest of the Promised Land, Moses asks God for a sign of his effective support, "Show me thy glory." God answers, "I will make all my goodness pass before you, and will proclaim before you my name 'The Lord' .... But you cannot see my face; for man shall not see me and live. Behold, there is a place by me where you shall stand upon the rock; and while my glory passes by I will put you in a cleft of the rock, and I will cover you with my hand until I have passed by; then I will take away my hand, and you shall see my back; but my face shall not be seen." (Exodus 33:19-23)

Nevertheless, it is better to do these kinds of readings of the divine providence very cautiously and to limit them to our personal lives. The notion of "divine providence" must not serve either to dispense people from their own responsibilities or to contradict human freedom. Indeed, the entire history of salvation demonstrates that human freedom is dearer to God than a desirable outcome of events. Likewise, the notion cannot be deployed to interpret another's misfortunes. This would bring us very close, indeed, to a retributive God, a God foreign to the Jewish-Christian tradition.

Praying with Sick Persons

The problem of suffering invites people to a personal (re-) vision of life, and the development of a hierarchy of values which is somewhat resistant to suffering. Suffering calls for an engagement, within which protest, solidarity, and consolation are given an appropriate place. Suffering also challenges us to pose the question of God again and again, and to remain "restless until we find rest in Him." All of this is not possible, however, if the believer does not live in a close relationship with God. Prayer and liturgy are among the most important means to promote and strengthen this relationship. In what follows, we shall reflect on one kind of prayer, namely, prayer with the sick, and on one kind of liturgical action, namely, the anointing of the sick.

In the past, prayer with sick persons was very nearly the exclusive prerogative of pastors and religious (especially sisters). Exceptions to this practice, such as cases of genuine emergency, were rare. This must change. One of the factors necessitating such a change is the rediscovery of the peculiar charism of the laity, a charism derived from their baptism and confirmation. All those who work in health care and come very close to the sick must help them in their prayer. Precisely because of their status as lay persons, and the "freelance" character of their involvement in pastoral work, the prayers of the laity can possess more appeal, for the sick, than the "official" prayers of professional pastoral workers.

The situation of a sick person is often an invitation to prayer. Many of the defense mechanisms which keep healthy people from prayer, are eliminated when sickness strikes. The sick person is profoundly aware of his or her needs, and is confronted with enormous questions of meaning. He or she feels longs for closeness. To pray is to ask for closeness.

The call for closeness can be expressed in different ways — sometimes not with words, but symbolically. Sick people sometimes talk hesitantly about their silent prayer: "I often look at the Cross. When I've done that, I can go on for a while." Or they have a statue of Mary or a rosary. A hospital chaplain recounts the following experience: "I knew a woman in the intensive care unit who had been clinging to her rosary for days; she would not let it go. It looked like she was clinging to her life. At the same time, she said, she prayed to be able to accept what was happening to her and to let go of her life. In all their insecurity, the sick may find some security in prayers." The director of a hospital told the following story of a thirty-five year old woman, who was dying: "In her hands she held a little purse, made by her twelve year old daughter as a gift for her last birthday. She kept a firm grip on it, the loop round her fingers. The fingers loosened at the moment of death. The process of attachment and release, as it finds place in leave-taking and dying, was symbolized by gripping and releasing the purse. It contained a photo of her husband and her children and a relic of Saint Rita. She held her concerns about her family close to her heart during the last moments of her life; her concern for her husband and her children, expressed in the photograph; and her awareness that her life was drawing to a close, expressed in the relic of Saint Rita, the patroness of lost causes."[29]

Often, prayer finds expression in words. The sick person prays, the pastor prays, the bystanders pray or lead the prayer. Prayers can be spontaneous, improvised, adapted to concrete circumstances. Texts can be used. There are many good books available.

In moments of great crisis, of desperation, finely-tuned words and well-balanced sentences can be inappropriate. In an emergency a compassionate helper may not be capable of improvisation. In such cases, very familiar prayers can often be employed, prayers such as the Our Father, or the Hail Mary, or brief refrains (of the sort used in Taizé). If something very familiar is prayed, such as the Our Father, it is often poignant to see how the patient tries to pray with the others, sometimes uttering only the first words, sometimes trailing somewhat behind, like an echo. This is much more important than beautifully crafted texts, read by one individual, before people whose capacity to listen is very limited. The bystanders — even if they have lost contact with the Church — can usually join in with relative ease. I have often seen weeping relatives become calmer when they were able to join in a familiar text. Prayers are not intended to stop the tears of those who mourn, though they may well do so.

The Bible is replete with prayers of petition. These prayers embrace an abundance of human concerns, and they are usually

[29] Emmanuel Keirse, *Wat meer is in de mens* (Leuven: Acco, 1985) 54-55.

formulated in a very direct fashion. They are the words of people who dare to speak to God on a one-to-one basis (the so-called *tutoyeurs de Dieu*). A brief reflection on the praying of the psalms can help us to discover the essence of supplication.

First of all, a psalm is a you-prayer. God is addressed in the most direct manner conceivable. The psalmist presupposes God's existence and His willingness to listen. People pray in all possible states. There is no diplomatic language in the psalms. Everyone addresses God in the light of the moment, giving vent to the feelings of the moment.

Once the contact is established — sometimes almost extorted: listen, unless you are deaf! — the story of suffering is told. Individual needs are aired, but these are never divorced from the needs of fellow humans. Sometimes the distress is mentioned only summarily; sometimes there is a detailed exposé about sickness, war, death, misery. Very often, the psalmist speaks of a problem with God Himself: "We don't understand you any longer. What will our enemies think of You?"

Then the arguments are expressed. From time to time, real challenges are thrown out: "Lord, you have done this and that for us, in the past, when you still were loveable!" Not seldom there is a sudden turning in the psalm, in the fashion of the passage from Hosea, which we discussed above. The sense of an alliance with God which will persist in spite of everything, prevails over the isolation of the sufferer. Immediately after this, often without any transition, the sufferer prays as if he or she were already heard. Based on former experiences and on the answer friends received, the supplicant presupposes that God has already saved him: "Weeping I went away and laughing I returned. It's now up to you, Lord." It is as if the psalmist confronts God with a *fait accompli*. Such a psalm-prayer ends with praise and thanksgiving, "I am so sure of Your intervention, that I thank You in advance. You are a God who saves."[30]

---

[30] See Psalm 22 and John 11:41: "Father I thank thee that thou hast heard me." Lazarus has not yet risen from the dead, but Jesus already thanks his Father.

Everything is allowed in prayers, as long as it is addressed, as long as the misery is worded in the vocative. The Bible hardly has a specific word for praying. To pray means to call, to shout, to laugh, to weep, to demand. It all depends on the circumstances. Everything is permitted; this is the most prominent feature of the relationship of this people with its God. Prayers need not be formulated in sacred, standardized words. One can pray in all possible positions and with all possible voices. The God of Israel differs from other gods, even here. Everything can be said to Him; no word is too spontaneous or too crude. You can play with Him; or flatter Him, as Abraham did when he negotiated on Sodom's behalf; or you can pour out your heart and rant and rave like Job.

The link between the psalms and the prayers of the sick is an obvious one. The prayers of the sick contain all kinds of emotions. At the first shock, prayers will cease. If there are feelings of anger and aggression, crude words, of the sort spoken by Job, will be used. Even in their prayers the sick will try to bargain. In periods of depression, the sick man or woman will themselves enter the garden of the Mount of Olives. Perhaps, on the way towards acceptance, psalm 23 will be possible, "The Lord is my shepherd," alternated with psalm 22, or the famous prayer of Charles de Foucauld (1858-1916), "I rely upon you because you are my Father."

A sick person will not always be capable of praying. People who have become isolated from the Church will not easily find appropriate words. In other cases, the pain is too heavy to allow prayer. At the Mount of Olives Jesus asked his friends to pray. Sometimes sick persons will ask, "Pray for me." Even apart from its religious significance, prayer for another is a powerful expression, and promise, of solidarity.

The most difficult question concerns the answer to our prayers.[31] In periods of distress, simply to have someone to talk with is a kind of being heard. A person ceases to be totally iso-

---

[31] Gisbert Greshake & Gerhard Lohfink (ed.), *Bittgebet - Testfall des Glaubens* (Mainz: Matthias Grünewald, 1978).

lated. A trouble shared is a trouble halved. The first step towards being answered is to be heard by God. However, a sick person is not always able to bring his or her sorrow before God. In deep suffering, he or she may not be capable of praying. Then, it falls to another to do it. In the New Testament, there are numerous examples of this sort of mediation and substitution.

But is there something more? Experience teaches us that not every prayer is heard, at least not in the fashion in which people would like it to be. God does not always remove the distressful situation. Nevertheless, if we pray with perseverance, He changes our attitude in the face of this distress. And this is a change in the distressful situation itself, since isolation makes distress as such even more hopeless. Where people can entrust their misery to a Father, they are protected from fatal despair. This was Jesus' experience at the Mount of Olives and on Golgotha. The situation is no less urgent, but it has been placed in a different context, and set against a background of hope. Perhaps not the hope of salvation during our earthly life, but, in any case, hope of eternal life. The worst death is not the death of the body. Here we encounter a claim that can only be a matter of faith. Christian hope unreservedly insists that to die means to be transformed like a grain of wheat. To be born again. The death to be afraid of is the Death of faith, of love, and of hope. Prayer always protects us from that Death.

Perhaps God does not give us precisely what we ask of Him. Perhaps His answer is profounder and more far-reaching than we realize, in view of His profounder view of what is really important. At the Mount of Olives Jesus asked to be liberated from Good Friday. His prayer was not granted. He received Easter. Perhaps human beings should give God the space Jesus gave his Father when He prayed, "Father, if thou art willing, remove this cup from me; nevertheless, not my will, but thine be done." (Luke 22:42)

To pray "in Jesus' name" (John 16:24) also means to pray like Jesus. It is to insist with confidence, to call the distress by its name, to ask for intercession, but always to conclude by saying,

"Your will be done." This is the only way to give new life a chance. It is the only way to give full play to God's creativity.

And here, God never fails. At the Mount of Olives "an angel appeared, strengthening him" (Luke 22:43). Assiduous prayer is allowed to expect signs of consolation and strengthening. Sometimes this can take the form of a real turn of events — one should not limit God's power. Sometimes His answer is an inner strengthening, which enables one to bear what must be borne. Sometimes it is the help offered by fellow humans. In any case, it is always consolation and strength. Nevertheless, even in petition, human beings are repeatedly confronted with a God who is "different" from the God they thought they knew. This is the final reason why no answer to the question of how our prayers are heard is ever completely satisfying.

The Anointing of the Sick

In every sacrament God gives "a sign of life" in the midst of the community of the faithful. The strongest Sign of Life is the Eucharist. Besides the Eucharist, there are two sacraments of faith, at the beginning of life, baptism and confirmation. There are two sacraments of love, where life becomes mission, matrimony and the sacrament of the orders. There are two sacraments of hope, when life has been wounded, reconciliation and the anointing of the sick.

Sacramental liturgy can never be detached from life. As far as anointing is concerned, the liturgical celebration is the condensation of all that people (the relatives, the friends, the medical personnel) have done and will do for the sick person. In this sense, the anointing can be called the divine seal on the care for the sick.

'To seal' is to do three things. In the first place, to seal is to authenticate. In the sacramental liturgy the pastor declares that everything that has been done to the sick person is the authentic work of God. Through human beings God has given signs of Life to the sufferer. In a certain sense, their dedication was an anointing. In the second place, to seal means to complete, to fulfil. The sacramental liturgy calls God by His name, explicitly, and calls Him upon in this situation. The liturgy transforms mute distress into a vocative. It very explicitly asks God to support this sick person. In the third place, to seal means to send. A seal serves to insure that a letter is sent. A sacrament is never a terminus. Even the anointing of the sick is a sacrament of mission. The anointed person is sent to be ointment to the wounds of other persons, even now.

The practice of the anointing of the sick is very ancient.[32] Traces of the practice can be found in the Gospels — among others, the anointing at Bethany by a woman (Mark 14:3-9; Matthew 26:6-13; John 12:1-8) — and in James 5:14-15. (Why do we almost exclusively quote the latter?) Since then, in varying forms, the community of the faithful has sought to care for the sick, not only by human support, but also by means of a guaranteed sign of God's presence.

During the first centuries (until about the 7th century), the oil for the sick was blessed by the bishop on Holy Thursday. The faithful took it home with them, as they did with holy water. Later on, the ointment became an unction *in extremis*. Its administration was reserved to priests and those who received the anointing were very close to death. Vatican II changed this practice. In a return to the more ancient tradition of the Church, extreme unction is now looked upon as the sacrament of the sick. This means that the sacrament can be celebrated with every baptized and confirmed Christian who is gravely ill, weakened by aging, or threatened by dangerous surgery. The anointing can be repeated when the illness is aggravated.

---

[32] Charles W. Gusmer, *And You Visited Me: Sacramental Ministry to the Sick and the Dying*, Studies in the Reformed Rites of the Catholic Church, VI (New York: Pueblo, 1984); *Pastoral Care of the Sick: Rites of Anointing and Viaticum: A Commentary (Collegeville: Liturgical Press, 1983)*; Bernhard Poschmann, *Penance and the Anointing of the Sick*, The Herder History of Dogma (New York: Herder and Herder, 1964); Herbert Vorgrimler, *Busse und Krankensalbung* (Freiburg: Herder, 1978); Gisbert Greshake, "Extreme Unction or Anointing of the Sick? A Plea for Discrimination," *Review for Religious* 45 (1986) 435-451; Peter E. Fink (ed.), *Anointing of the Sick*, Alternative Futures for Worship, 7 (Collegeville: Liturgical Press, 1987)

Except in the case of emergencies, the anointing is celebrated within the framework of a particular liturgical celebration or a Eucharist. At the beginning, the priest blesses the sick person with water, which is intended to recall our baptism. If the sick person so desires, he or she can receive the sacrament of reconciliation. In other cases, all the bystanders are invited to participate in a penitential rite. A text from the Bible is read. Then the pastor and the bystanders lay their hands on the sick person. Their familiar faces, their quiet prayer, their closeness, all express God's nearness and His concern for this sick person. This laying on of hands is a gesture of protection and encouragement, and a demand for the coming of the Spirit of true consolation.

Then the priest anoints the sick person. This is God's anointing; His appeasing presence pervades the sick person. Oil is a symbol of the Spirit. Jesus is the Anointed One. The Spirit transforms the sufferer and makes him or her more 'like unto Christ': "Through this holy anointing may the Lord in His love and mercy help you with the grace of the Holy Spirit. May the Lord who frees you from sin save you and raise you up."

"To be saved and raised up." This text fundamentally alters the meaning given to the former practice of extreme unction, which heavily stressed the forgiveness of the sins committed by the different senses. The key words of this renewed rite are "to save" and to "raise up."

Salvation is a word with many different meanings. The meaning it possesses in a concrete case must ultimately be determined by God. It cannot be filled in by human beings. Sometimes a sick person will recover. Most often, he or she feels better. The body and the spirit are inextricably linked. The sick person will feel more tranquil. By the anointing he or she has been related to God and to his or her fellows. Closeness and hope are powerful realities.

Still, the anointing also aims at a more profound healing. God will stand by the sick person, even if he or she dies, now or later. God will heal the sick, to eternal life. He will raise them up. In every sense of the word. One day they will come home. One day it will be Easter for the sick person — because God is reliable.

CONCLUSION: AN EASTER MESSAGE

Like the other sacraments, the anointing of the sick is an Easter message. In the case of the anointing, the Easter message is addressed very concretely to the situation of conflict within which the sick person finds himself or herself. This sacrament gives very clear expression to the central ideas of this book.

In the first part we described the fourfold conflict aroused by sickness: the conflict with the body, with the world, with fellow humans, and with finiteness. When serious illness strikes, these conflicts become decisive, *crucial*. From the perspective of faith, what is "crucial" cannot be conceived or approached apart from the Cross. It is only by applying the Cross to his or her situation that the sufferer can find release. Such an application means at least three things.

In the first place, the sick person realizes that he or she is not alone in his or her suffering. The liturgy of the sick puts the suffering person in a relationship with the crucified Christ. Christ, too, has lived the fourfold conflict. Christ's way of the cross was a conflict with his body, until he fell under the Cross. Jesus experienced the conflict with his environment; the soldiers cast lots for his garments. As his disciples withdrew, he faced growing isolation. He fought the last fight with his Father on Golgotha.

In the second place, the memory of Christ's Cross is the memory of how Jesus has been saved and healed. The liturgy of the sick symbolizes how Jesus grew through these conflicts to a new harmony. After his resurrection his body is the same, but the wounds no longer bleed. In the tomb he receives new garments, white ones, symbols of the final victory. The increasing isolation turns into a renewed alliance. The centrifugal movement changes into a centripetal one, the creation of new communities. The experience of being abandoned by God turns into an experience of God's nearness, "Into thy hands."

In the third place, the Cross and the liturgy of the sick are both an Easter message, the promise that the sick person, too, will be healed to a new harmony. Christ's example would be completely powerless if it were nothing but the story of somebody "who made it." With words and gestures the anointing promises, "in the name of the Lord," that the sick person will "make the passage" from death to fulfillment.

Why? Because the mystery of Mercy is stronger than the mystery of evil.

BIBLIOGRAPHY

Alberton, M., *Un sacrement pour les malades dans le contexte actuel de la santé*, Paris, Le Centurion, 1978.

Amato, J. A., Monge, D., Weber, E., *Victims and Values: A History and a Theory of Suffering*, Westport (Conn.), Greenwood Reprint Corporation, 1990.

Aries, P., *Western Attitudes toward Death from the Middle-Ages to the Present*, Baltimore, John Hopkins University Press, 1974.

Aries, P., *L'Homme devant la Mort*, Paris, Seuil, 1977.

Barineau, R. M., *The Theodicy of Alfred North Whitehead: A Logical and Ethical Vindication*, Lanham (Md.), University Press of America, 1991.

Barth, H.-M., "Angesichts des Leiden von Gott reden," *Pastoraltheologie* 75 (1986) 116-131.

Beker, J. Chr., *Suffering And Hope: The Biblical Vision and the Human Predicament*, Philadelphia, Fortress Press, 1987.

Berger, M. & Hortala, Fr., *Mourir à l'hôpital*, Paris, Le Centurion, 1984.

Boff, L., *Passion of Christ, Passion of the World: The Facts, their Interpretation and their Meaning Yesterday and Today*, New York, Orbis, 1987.

Bonhöffer, D., *Letters and Papers from Prison*, London, SCM, 1973.

Borsch, Fr. H., *Power in Weakness: New Hearing for Gospel Stories of Healing and Discipleship*, Philadelphia, Fortress Press, 1983.

Bowker, J., *Problems of Suffering in Religions of the World*, London, Cambridge University Press, 1975.

Brantschen, J. B., "Leiden. Theologische Perspektiven," *Christlicher Glaube in moderner Gesellschaft*, band 10, Freiburg, Herder, 1980, 37-47.

Brantschen, J. B., *Warum lässt der gute Gott uns leiden?*, Freiburg im Breisgau, Herder, 1986.

Burkle, H.R., *God, Suffering & Belief*, Nashville, Abington, 1977.

Carretto, C., Barr, R., *Why O Lord? The Inner Meaning of Suffering*, Maryknoll (N.Y.), Orbis books, 1986.

Chopp, Rebecca S., *The Praxis of Suffering: An Interpretation of Liberation and Political Theologies*, Maryknoll (N.Y.), Orbis books, 1986.

Clift, J. D., *Core Images of the Self: A Symbolic Approach to Healing and Wholeness*, New York, Crossroad, 1992.

Cobb, J.B., *God and the World*, Philadelphia, Westminster, 1969.

Cowburn, J., *Shadows and the Dark: The Problems of Suffering and Evil*, London, SCM, 1979.

Creel, R.E., *Divine Impassibility: An Essay in Philosophical Theology*, Cambridge, Cambridge University Press, 1986.

Daniel, Amy, *Towards a Theology of Healing and Wholeness*, Leuven, Catholic University, Faculty of Theology, Diss. Ph. D. in Religious Studies, 1993.

Danneels, G., *Pas de dimanche sans vendredi: croix, souffrance et sacrifice*, Mechelen, Service de presse de l'Archevêché, 1992.

Davis, S.T., (ed.) *Encountering Evil: Live Options in Theodicy*, Atlanta, John Knox, 1981.

de Halleux, A., "Dieu le Père tout-puissant," in *Revue Théologique de Louvain* 8 (1977) 401-422.

Delumeau, J., *Sin and Fear: the Emergence of a Western Guilt Culture, 13th-18th century*, New York, Saint Martins Press, 1990.

DePender, W., Ikeda-Chandler, Wanda, *Clinical Ethics: An Invitation to Healing Professionals*, New York, Praeger, 1990.

Depoortere, K., "Mal et Libération. Une étude de l'oeuvre de Paul Ricoeur," *Studia Moralia* 14 (1976) 337-385.

Depoortere, K., "You Have Striven with God," A Pastoral-Theological Reflection on the Image of God and Suffering," in Lambrecht, J. & Collins, R. (ed.), *God and Human Suffering* (Louvain Theological & Pastoral Monographs 3), Leuven, Peeters, 1990, 211-234.

De Schrijver, G., "Theodicy, Justification and Justice," *Archivio di Filosofia* 56 (1988) 291-310.

Despland, M., *Kant on History and Religion*, Montreal and London, McGill - Queen's University Press, 1973.

Dougherty, F., *The Meaning of Human Suffering*, New York, Human Sciences Press, 1982.

Duquoc, Chr., "The Folly of the Cross and 'the Human'," *Concilium* 155 (1982) no. 5, 65-73.

Duquoc, Chr., Floristan, C. (ed.), *Job and the Silence of God*, *Concilium* 169 (1983) no. 9.

Durand, G. & Malherbe, J.-Fr., *Vivre avec la souffrance: repères théologiques*, Montréal, Fides, 1992.

Eibach, U., "Die Sprache leidender Menschen und der Wandel des Gottesbildes," *Theologische Zeitschrift* 40 (1984) 34-65.

Eigo, Fr. A., *Whither Creativity, Freedom, Suffering: Humanity, Cosmos, God*, Villanova, Villanova University Press, 1981.

Elphinstone, A., *Freedom, Suffering and Love*, London, SCM, 1976.

Empereur, J. L., *Prophetic Anointing: God's Call to the Sick, the Elderly, and the Dying*, Wilmington (Delaware), Glazier, 1982.

Engelke, E., *Sterbenskranke und die Kirche*, Munich, Kaiser, 1980.

Estadt, B.K., Compton, J. R., Blanchette, M.C., *The Art of Clinical Supervision: A Pastoral Counseling Perspective*, New York, Paulist Press, 1987.

Evely, L., Thompson, Marie-Claude, *Suffering*, New York, Herder and Herder, 1967.

Fasselt, G., *Die gemeinsame Sorge von Arzt und Seelsorger für die Kranken*, Mainz, Matthias Grünewald, 1987.

Fiddes, P. S., *The Creative Suffering of God*, Oxford, Clarendon, 1988.

Fink, P.E. (ed.), *Anointing of the Sick*, Collegeville, Liturgical Press, 1987.

Fiorenza, F.P., "Joy and Pain as Paradigmatic for Language about God," *Concilium* 10 (1974) no. 5, 67-80.

Foskett, J., *Meaning in Madness: The Pastor and the Mentally Ill*, London, SPCK, 1984.

Frankenberry, Nancy, "Some Problems in Process Theodicy," *Religious Studies* 17 (1981) 179-197.

Frankl, V., *Man's Search for Meaning: An Introduction to Logotherapy*, New York, Pocket Books, 1963.

Frankl, V., *The Unconscious God: Psychotherapy and Theology*, New York, Simon and Schuster, 1975.

Frankl, V., *Das Leiden am sinnlosen Leben: Psychotherapie für heute*, Freiburg, Herder, 1977.

Fretheim, T. E., *The Suffering of God: an Old Testament Perspective*, Philadelphia, Fortress Press, 1984.

Galipeau, S. A., *Transforming Body and Soul: Therapeutic Wisdom in the Gospel Healing Stories*, New York, Paulist Press, 1990.

Galot, P., *Dieu souffre-t-il?*, Paris, Lethielleux, 1976.

Gerstenberger, E.S., Schrage, W., *Suffering*, Nashville, Abingdon, 1977.

Gesché, A., "Topiques de la question du mal," *Revue Théologique de Louvain* 17 (1986) 393-418.

Gesché, A., "Odyssée de la théodicée. Dieu dans l'objection," *Archivio di Filosofia* 56 (1988) 453-468.

Gielen, H. & Nackaerts, F., *Stauros Bibliography: Human Suffering and Christ's Passion; Bibliographie Stauros: souffrance humaine et passion du Christ*, Leuven, Stauros, 1. 1972-73; 2. 1974-75; 3. 1976-77; 4. 1978-79; 5. 1980-81; 6. 1982-83; 7. 1984-85; 8. 1986-87; 9. 1988-89.

Glaser, B.G., & Strauss, A.L., *Awareness of Dying*, Chicago, Aldine Publishing Co., 1965.

Gonnet, D., *Dieu aussi connaît la souffrance*, Paris, Cerf, 1990.

Grassi, J. A., *Healing the Heart: The Transformational Power of Biblical Heart Imagery*, New York, Paulist Press, 1987.

Gray, J., Thompson, R. F., *Traditional Religion and Healing in Sub-Saharan Africa and the Diaspora: A Classified International Bibliography*, Westport (Conn.), Greenwood Press, 1989.

Greshake, G., "Suffering and the Question of God," *Stauros Bulletin*, no. 1 (1977) 3-32 (Original: "Leiden und Gottesfrage," *Geist und Leben* 50 (1977) 102-120.

Greshake, G., *Der Preis der Liebe. Besinnung über das Leid*, Freiburg im Breisgau, Herder, 1979; Revised edition, *Wenn Leid mein Leben lahmt: Leiden, Preis der Liebe?*, Freiburg im Breisgau, Herder, 1992.

Greshake, G. & Lohfink, G. (ed.), *Bittgebet - Testfall des Glaubens*, Mainz, Matthias Grünewald, 1978.

Greshake, G., "Extreme Unction or Anointing of the Sick? A Plea for Discrimination," *Review for Religious* 45 (1986) 435-451.

Griffin, D, *God, Power and Evil. A Process Theodicy*, Philadelphia, Westminster, 1976.

Gusmer, Ch. W., *And You Visited Me: Sacramental Ministry to the Sick and the Dying*, New York, Pueblo, 1984.

Gutierrez, G., O'Connell, M. J., *On Job: God-talk and the Suffering of the Innocent*, Maryknoll (N.Y.), Orbis books, 1987.

Hall, D.J., *God and Human Suffering: An Exercise in the Theology of the Cross*, Minneapolis, Augsburg, 1986.

Häring, H., "Het kwaad als vraag naar Gods almacht en machteloos-heid," *Tijdschrift voor Theologie* 26 (1986) 351-372.

Harper, A. W. J., *The Theodicy of Suffering*, San Francisco (Calif.), Mellen Research Univ. Press, 1990.

Hartshorne, C., *Omnipotence and other Theological Mistakes*, Albany (N.Y.), State University of New York Press, 1984.

Hauerwas, St., *Suffering Presence: Theological Reflections on Medicine, the Mentally Handicapped and the Church*, Edinburgh, Clark, 1988.

Hauerwas St., *Naming the Silences: God, Medicine, and the Problem of Suffering*, Grand Rapids (Mich.), Eerdmans, 1990.

Hebblethwaite, Br., *Evil, Suffering and Religion*, London, Sheldon, 1976.

Hedinger, U., *Wider die Versöhnung Gottes mit dem Elend. Eine Kritik des christlichen Theismus und A-Theismus*, Zürich, Theologischer Verlag, 1972.

Hick, J., *Evil and the God of Love*, London, Macmillan, 2nd edit., 1977.

International Committee on English in the Liturgy, *Pastoral Care of the Sick: Introduction and Pastoral Notes*, Washington, United States Catholic Conference, 1983, 64 p.

Hong H.V. & Hong E.H., (ed.), *Soren Kierkegaard's Journals and Papers*, Bloomington and London, Indiana University Press, 7 vol., 1967-1978.

Jackson, E. N., *The Role of Faith in the Process of Healing*, London, SCM, 1981.

John Paul II, *Salvifici doloris: On the Christian Meaning of Human Suffering* (United States Catholic Conference Publications 919), 1984, 40 p.; ID, in *Origins* 13 (1984) 609-624.

Jüngel, E., *God as the Mystery of the World: On the Foundation of the Theology of the Crucified One in the Dispute between Theism and Atheism*, Grand Rapids (Mi.) Eerdmans, 1983.

Kamp, J., *Souffrance de Dieu, vie du monde*, Tournai, Casterman, 1971.

Kasper, W., "Anthropologische Aspekte der Busse," *Theologische Quartalschrift* 163 (1983) 96-109.

Kastenbaum R., & Costa, "Psychological Perspectives on Death," *Annual Review of Psychology* 28 (1977) 225-249.

Keirse, E., *Wat meer is in de mens*, Leuven, Acco, 1985.

Kelsey, M. T., *Healing and Christianity in Ancient Thought and Modern Times*, New York (N.Y.), Harper and Row, 1973.

King, J. N., *The God of Forgiveness and Healing in the Theology of Karl Rahner*, Washington, University Press of America, 1982.

Kitamori, K., *Theology of the Pain of God*, London, SCM, 1966.

Kleinman, A., *The Illness Narratives: Suffering, Healing, and the Human Condition*, New York, Basic books, 1988.

Kübler-Ross, Elizabeth, *On Death and Dying*, New York, Macmillan Company, 1969.

Kübler-Ross, Elizabeth, *Death, the Final Stage of Growth*, Englewood Cliffs, Prentice-Hall, 1975.

Küng, H., *Gott und das Leid*, Einsiedeln, Benziger, 1967.

Küng, H., "Die Religionen als Frage an die Theologie des Kreuzes," *Evangelische Theologie* 33 (1973) 401-423.

Küng, H., *Eternal Life?*, London, Collins / New York, Doubleday, 1984.

Kushner, H. S., *When Bad Things Happen to Good People*, New York, Avon Books, 1983.

Lack, S. & Lamerton, R.(ed.), *The Hour of our Death*, Londen, Geoffrey Chapman, 1974.

Lactantius, *The Wrath of God*, in *Lactantius: The Minor Works*, Washington, The Catholic University of America Press, 1965.

Lambrecht, J. & Collins, R., (ed.), *God and Human Suffering*, Leuven, Peeters, 1990.

Lee, J.Y., *God Suffers For Us. A Systematic Inquiry into a Concept of Divine Passibility*, The Hague, Martinus Nijhoff, 1974.

Lehmann, K., *Jesus Christus ist auferstanden*, Freiburg, Herder, 1975.

Leibniz, G.W., *Essais de Théodicée sur la bonté de Dieu, la liberté de l'homme et l'origine du mal*, 1710. English translation: Allen D., (ed.), *Theodicy*, Ontario, J. Dent & Sons, 1966.

Levinas, E., "La souffrance inutile," *Giornale di Metafisica* 4 (1982) 13-25.

Liderbach, D., *Why do we Suffer? New Ways of Understanding*, New York, Paulist Press, 1992.

MacDermott, J. M., *The Bible on Human Suffering*, Slough, St Paul Publications, 1990.

MacGill, A., Ramsey, P., *Suffering: A Test of Theological Method*, Philadelphia, Westminster Press, 1982.

MacNutt, Fr., *Healing*, Notre Dame (Ind.), Ave Maria Press, 4th edit., 1975.

MacWilliams, W., *The Passion of God: Divine Suffering in Contemporary Protestant Theology*, Macon, Mercer University Press, 1985.

Madre, Ph., Coffy, R., *La guérison extraordinaire existe-t-elle?*, Paris, Ed. Breg, 1982.

Madre, Ph., *Souffrance des hommes et compassion de Dieu. 1: Le scandale du mal*, Nouan-le-Fuzelier, édit. du Lion de Juda, 1990.

Manigne, J.-P., *Peut-on parler de la souffrance?*, Paris, Desclée De Brouwer, 1991.

Martelet, G., *Libre réponse à un scandale: la faute originelle, la souffrance et la mort*, Paris, Cerf, 5th edit., 1992.

Metz, J.B., "The Future in the Memory of Suffering," *Concilium* 8 (1972) no. 6, 9-25.

Molinié, M.D., *Le courage d'avoir peur*, Paris, Cerf, 1975.

Moltmann, J. *The Crucified God: The Cross of Christ as the Foundation and Criticism of Christian Theology*, London, SCM, 1974.

Moltmann, J., "The Motherly Father: Is Trinitarian Patripassianism Replacing Theological Patriarchalism?," *Concilium* 143 (1981) no. 3, 51-56.

Moltmann, J., *Trinität und Reich Gottes. Zur Gotteslehre*, Munich, Kaiser, 1980.

Moltmann, J., *Gott in der Schöpfung. Ökologische Schöpfungslehre*, Munich, Kaiser, 1985.

Morse, Janice M., Johnson, J. L., *The Illness Experience: Dimensions of Suffering*, Newbury Park (Calif.), Sage, 1991.

Murphree, J. T., *A Loving God and a Suffering World: A New Look at an Old Problem*, Downers Grove (Ill.), Intervarsity Press, 1981.

Nemo, P., *Job et l'excès du mal*, Paris, Grasset, 1978.

Nouwen, H., *The Wounded Healer: Ministry in Contemporary Society*, New York, Doubleday & Company, 1972.

O'Connell, T., *What a Modern Catholic Believes about Suffering and Evil*, Chicago, Th.More, 1972.

Ortemann, Cl., *Le sacrement des malades: histoire et signification*, Lyon, Chalet, 1971.

Ortemann, Cl., "Quelle parole chrétienne sur la souffrance?," *Lumen Vitae* 37 (1982) 295-308.

Permanent Council of the French Episcopal Conference, "Respecting the Person Close to Death" (23 September 1991), *Catholic International* 2 (1991), no. 19, 1-14 November 1991, 909-916.

Perrin, L., Simon, R., *Guérir et sauver: entendre la parole des malades*, Paris, Cerf, 1987.

Peterson, M.L., "Recent Work on the Problem of Evil," *American Philosophical Quarterly* 20 (1983) 321-339.

Philips, D.Z., "On Not Understanding God," *Archivio di Filosofia* 56 (1988) 597-612.

Poschmann, B., *Penance and the Anointing of the Sick*, New York, Herder, 1964.

Probst, M., Richter, Kl., *Heilssorge für die Kranken, und Hilfen zur Erneuerung eines missverstandenen Sakraments*, Freiburg, Herder, 1975.

Rahner, K., *Bergend und heilend: über das Sakrament der Kranken*, Munich, Ars sacra, 1965.

Rahner, K., "Why Does God Allow Us to Suffer?," *Theological Investigations 19*, New York, Crossroad, 1983, 194-208.

Reichenbach, B.R., *Evil and a Good God*, New York, Fordham University Press, 1982.

Richard, L., *What Are They Saying about the Theology of Suffering?*, New York, Paulist Press, 1992.

Ricoeur, P., *The Symbolism of Evil*, Boston, Beacon, 1969.

Ricoeur, P., "Evil: a Challenge to Philosophy and Theology," in Deuser, H., Martin, G.M., Stock, K., Welker M., (ed.), *Gottes Zukunft - Zukunft der Welt. Festschrift für Jürgen Moltmann zum 60. Geburtstag*, Munich, Kaiser, 1986, 345-361.

Schattner, M., *Souffrance et dignité humaine: pour une médicine de la personne*, Paris, Mame, 1993.

Schillebeeckx, E., "The Mystery of Injustice and the Mystery of Mercy. Questions Concerning Human Suffering," *Stauros Bulletin*, no. 3 (1975) 3-31. (Original: "Mysterie van ongerechtigheid en mysterie van erbarmen. Vragen rond het menselijk lijden," *Tijdschrift voor Theologie* 15 (1975) 3-25.

Shlemon, Barbara L., Linn, D., Linn, M., *To Heal as Jesus Healed*, Notre Dame (Ind.), Ave Maria Press, 1976.

Shlemon, Barbara L., MacNutt, Fr., *Healing Prayer*, Notre Dame (Ind.), Ave Maria Press, 1976.

Simon, L., *Einstellungen und Erwartungen der Patienten im Krankenhaus gegenüber dem Seelsorger*, Frankfurt a. M., Lang, 1985.

Sölle, Dorothee, *Suffering*, Philadelphia, Fortress Press, 1984.

Sparn, W., *Leiden - Erfahrungen und Denken. Materialien zum Theodizeeproblem*, Munich, Kaiser, 1980.

Sporken, P., *Heb jij aanvaard dat ik sterven moet?*, Baarn, Ambo, 1981.

Stanley, D. M., *Jesus in Gethsemane: the Early Church Reflects on the Suffering of Jesus*, New York (N.Y.), Paulist Press, 1980.

Steen, M., "The Theme of the 'Suffering' God: An Exploration," J. Lambrecht & R., Collins, *God and Human Suffering*, Leuven, Peeters, 1990, p.69-93.

Surin, K., *Theology and the Problem of Evil*, Oxford, Basil Blackwell, 1986.

Taylor, M. J.(ed.), *The Mystery of Suffering and Death*, Staten Island (N.Y.), Alba house, 1973.

Taylor, M. J., "Theodicy and Religious Education," *Religious Education* 84 (1984) 5-76.

Teilhard de Chardin, P., *The Phenomenon of Man*, London, Collins, 1965.

Thévenot, X., *Souffrance, bonheur, éthique: conférences spirituelles*, Mulhouse, Salvator, 1990.

Thilo, H.-J., *Die therapeutische Funktion des Gottesdienstes*, Kassel, Stauda, 1985.

Tilley, T. W., *The Evils of Theodicy*, Washington, Georgetown University Press, 1991.

Tillich, P., *The Courage to Be*, London, Collins, 1952.

Tournier, P., *Face à la souffrance*, Genève, Labor et Fides, 1985.

van den Berg, J. H., *Psychologie van het ziekbed*, Nijkerk, Callenbach, 1952.

Van Den Bussche, H., "De ballade der miskende liefde," *Collationes Brugenses et Gandavenses* 4 (1958) 434-466.

Van der Veken, J., *God and Change: Process Thought and the Christian Doctrine of God*, Leuven, Center for Metaphysics and Philosophy of God, 1987.

van der Ven, J.A., "Theodicy or Cosmodicy: a False Dilemma?," *Journal of Empirical Theology* 2 (1989) 5-27.

van der Zee, W. R., *Wie heeft daar woorden voor? Een pastorale over lijdende mensen en een leidende God*, 's Gravenhage, Boekencentrum, 1981.

Vanhoutte, J., "God as Companion and Fellow-sufferer: An Image Emerging from Process Thought," *Archivio di Filosofia* 56 (1988) 191-225.

Varillon, Fr., *La souffrance de Dieu*, Paris, Le Centurion, 1976.

Varillon, Fr., *Beauté du monde et souffrance des hommes*, Paris, Le Centurion, 1980.

Varone, Fr., *Ce Dieu censé aimer la souffrance*, Paris, Cerf, 1984.

Vergote, A., *Het meerstemmige leven. Gedachten over mens en religie*, Kapellen, Pelckmans, 1987.

Vergote, A., *Guilt and Desire: Religious Attitudes and Their Pathological Derivatives*, New Haven, Yale University Press, 1988.

Vetter, H., *Der Schmerz und die Würde des Persons*, Frankfurt, J. Knecht, 1980.

Vimort, J., *Ensemble face à la mort. Accompagnement spirituel*, Paris, Le Centurion, 1987.

Vorgrimler, H., *Busse und Krankensalbung*, Freiburg, Herder, 2nd edit., 1978.

Walsh, J.& P., *Divine Providence and Human Suffering*, Wilmington (Delaware), Glazier, 1985.

Weil, S., *La Pesanteur et la Grâce*, Paris, Plon, 1948.

Wiersinga, H., *Verzoening met het lijden?*, Baarn, Ten Have, 1975.

Wiesel, E., *Night*, New York, Hill and Wang, 1960.

Wildes, K., *Birth, Suffering and Death: Catholic Perspectives at the Edges of Life*, Dordrecht, Kluwer Academic publ., 1992.

Wilkinson, J., *Health and Healing: Studies in New Testament Principles and Practices*, Edinburgh, Handsel Press, 1980.

Wilson, M., *The Church is Healing*, Londen, SCM, 1966.

Winkler, E., "Die Frage nach dem Sinn des Leidens in der Seelsorge," *Theologische Literaturzeitung* 104 (1979) 81-94.

Zahrnt, H., *Wie kann Gott das zulassen? Hiob - Der Mensch im Leid*, Munich, Piper, 1985.

Zenger, E., *Durchkreuztes Leben*, Freiburg, Herder, 1976.

Zenger, E., "Leiden. Biblische perspektiven," in *Christlicher Glaube in moderner Gesellschaft*, band 10, Freiburg, Herder, 1980, p. 27-36.